# THE WORLD OF
# PHILIP
### AND
# ALEXANDER

University Museum Public Forum Series I

# THE WORLD OF
# PHILIP
## AND
# ALEXANDER

*A Symposium on Greek Life and Times*

Elin C. Danien, Editor

*Published by*

THE UNIVERSITY MUSEUM
OF ARCHAEOLOGY AND ANTHROPOLOGY
University of Pennsylvania
1990

**Design**
Dennis Roberts

**Editing, production**
Publications Department
The University Museum

**Printing**
Science Press
Ephrata, Pennsylvania

**Library of Congress Cataloging-in-Publication Data**

The World of Philip and Alexander   :    a symposium on Greek life and
  times   /   Elin C. Danien, editor.
        p.    cm.   --  (University Museum public forum series   ;   1)
     "Originally ... presented as lectures at a symposium for the
  public at The University Museum of Archaeology and Anthropology in
  Philadelphia"--Foreword.
     Includes bibliographical references (p.     ).
     ISBN 0-934718-94-6
     1. Greece--History--Macedonian Expansion, 359-323--Congresses.
  2. Philip II. King of Macedonia, 382-336 B.C.--Congresses.
  3. Alexander, the Great, 358-323 B.C.--Congresses.    I. Danien, Elin
  C.   II. University of Pennsylvania.    University Museum of
  Archaeology and Anthropology.    III. Series.
  DF233.W67     1990
  938'.07--dc20                                                   90-24084
                                                                       CIP

# Table of Contents

# FIGURES

*FOREWORD*

The magnetism of the man known as Alexander the Great is almost a tangible substance, felt by people in all times since that brilliant young Macedonian conquered his world over two thousand years ago. Scholars whose fields touch that power continue to be intrigued by the man and the ways in which his actions altered or significantly contributed to Western culture. Here, each author, not necessarily a specialist in a field centered on Alexander, has nonetheless felt this fascination. Each was asked to look at the fourth century B.C. from his or her particular vantage, whether it was war, religion, state-craft, intrigue, or the central and symbolic role of the Greek games. This approach throws light not only on Alexander, but on the larger world within which he moved, and on areas where his efforts may have had a more oblique effect.

Originally, these articles were presented as lectures at a symposium for the public at The University Museum of Archaeology and Anthropology in Philadelphia. As a vital part of the University of Pennsylvania, the Museum is involved in the education of future scholars. From its earliest days, it has also maintained a commitment to bring to the interested public the scholarly research that is the heart of its efforts. Whether through lectures, films, or the innovative television series of the fifties *What in the World?* it has sought to bring to the public the results of its own research and that of institutions all over the world. Beginning in 1982, during my tenure as Coordinator of Public Programs, and with the support and guidance of Dr. Robert H. Dyson, Jr., Director, The University Museum initiated a series of one- and two-day symposia to further broaden its public stance. Each symposium brought together outstanding scholars to speak on current research, discuss controversial theories, and explore with the interested public the many fascinating byways of the past. Several of these symposia have provided the topics for special thematic issues of *Expedition*, the Museum's award winning magazine (for example, Archaeology and the History of Farming (28 [2] 1986); Discovery of Maya History (27 [3] 1985); and Archaeology Facts and Fantasies (29 [2] 1987). Now, this publication adds another dimension to the public outreach of the Museum.

At a time when Americans enjoy more years of leisure, when retirement comes earlier, and life expectancy is longer, the concept of "lifelong learning" should be much more than an empty slogan. The coming together of scholars and the interested public in arenas such as this publication and the symposium that engendered it, can suggest a model for learning beyond the walls of the university classroom. The delight of the speakers in encountering a large, interested, intelligent audience will help, I trust, in breaking down the traditional mistrust between "scholar" and "popularizer," in dispensing with the somewhat artificial separation of "student" and "amateur," and in fostering an atmosphere in which all are united in a quest for knowledge for its own sake.

This publication could not have succeeded without the efforts of the production staff for this project. Deborah Stuart was in charge of the preliminary editing and Kathy Moreau undertook the final editing and typesetting. The design concept and its production was carried out by Dennis Roberts. Karen Vellucci, Coordinator of Publications, oversaw the myriad tasks required to bring the project to a successful close. My appreciation for their talents and good nature grows with time. And, most emphatically, I thank the speakers cum authors, who responded positively to every request and thoughtfully shared their knowledge.

I also wish to express my gratitude to Dr. Spiros Iakovidis, Curator of the Mediterranean Section, who was an encouraging presence at all times. As discussion moderator, his wit and urbanity were much appreciated.

It is my hope that the following pages will fulfill one ancient Greek definition of a symposium, that of a convivial meeting for intellectual discussion.

*Elin C. Danien*

# I

# The Historical
Significance of
Philip of Macedon

*A.J. Graham*

$P$HILIP OF MACEDON, also called Philip II, the father of Alexander the Great—for we need not be led astray by the tale put about by those promoting the idea of Alexander's divinity, that Alexander was engendered by Zeus, who visited his mother, Olympias, in the form of a snake—was born in 383 or 382 B.C. to the then king of Macedon, Amyntas III, and Eurydice, one of his two known wives. Philip spent two or three years in his teens as a hostage in Thebes, when Macedon was in a state of great weakness during the reigns of his older brothers, Alexander II and Pediccas III. In 359 B.C. his own rule over Macedon began; it ended with his assassination in 336 B.C.

During these twenty-three years he took Macedon from a weak, divided, and threatened state to such military and political pre-eminence that he could undertake war against the Persian Empire, then the greatest power in the world. Such an achievement in war and politics inspires awe. Without it, the much better known career of his son is unthinkable. Yet Philip remains completely overshadowed by Alexander's world renown, a historical figure relatively little known and little admired. The reason for this lies partly in the character of the historical sources for his career.

No contemporary narrative history has survived, and we are therefore dependent on much later, and generally undistinguished, historians. More important, most of our contemporary information comes from the speeches of his most famous opponent, Demosthenes of Athens, the most admired orator of the ancient world. In the powerfully eloquent phrases of Demosthenes, Philip is the ambitious and unscrupulous enemy, who deprived the ancient city-states of Greece, and Athens above all, of their cherished freedom. For all later students of Ancient Greece, for whom Greek literature was the classical model and guide, the picture of Philip was inevitably unfavorable.

In recent years, there has been quite a spate of publications which seek to redress the balance, to depict Philip's career from a Macedonian viewpoint, and to advocate Philip's claims to admiration (Ellis 1976; Cawkwell 1978; Griffith in Hammond and Griffith 1979). Their Philip is given full credit for his mastery of military and political strategy, and Demosthenes' many weaknesses are, by contrast, mercilessly exposed. There is no doubt that such a correction of the historical interpretation is salutary, whether or not it is judged to be fully convincing, and it should enable us to achieve a better assessment of the historical significance of Philip of Macedon.

The Greek world which Philip was to subjugate consisted largely of numerous individual city-states, with relatively small territories and populations (map 1). The relations between these city-states were often hostile and wars were common. By the fourth century B.C. many of these states had long and proud histories of great achievements in war and peace which nourished their intense local patriotism. Historical developments, and particularly military developments, had made it impossible, however, for even the greatest of them, such as Athens, or Thebes, or Sparta, to protect their security by their own forces alone. As a result, various interstate organizations were created, such as federal leagues or large alliances under the leadership of one great state. Such organizations, however, tended to be inherently unstable because they encroached on the independence which the individual cities valued so highly. So, side by side with these developments, there were also many attempts to establish general peace and autonomy for

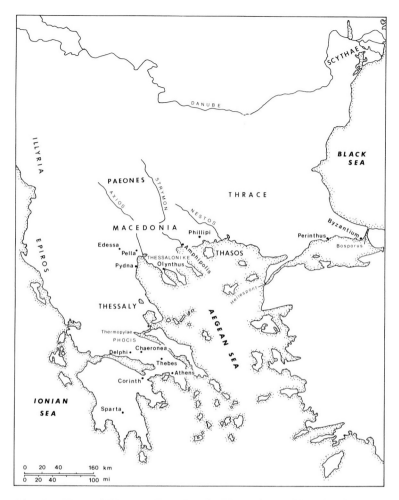

Fig. 1.  Map of Greece. *Drawing by Georgianna Grentzenberg.*

all Greek states (Ryder 1965). But all these attempts quickly foundered owing to the imperialistic ambitions of the greater powers. By the time that Philip appeared on the scene, there was no true peace and no one state was dominant. So, with the benefit of hindsight, we can see that the Greek world was divided and weak. No one at the time, however, could have foreseen that it would be threatened by Macedon.

5

The country of Macedonia consists of extensive alluvial plains at the mouths of its great rivers (Lower Macedonia), and of many smaller, but equally fertile, plains lying at high altitudes between the mountains (Upper Macedonia). Such a country was rich agriculturally and able to support, by Greek standards, a large population (though we can only make a very approximate guesses of its size).

Who were the people called the Macedonians? Questions of racial affinity are notoriously difficult to answer, especially when, as here, no simple political test can be applied. The ethnic ascription of the Macedonians has provoked debate since Antiquity, especially because it has been bedeviled by nationalist attitudes and hostilities. Thus, it had usually been put in the form, Were the Macedonians Greeks? Of the tests that can be applied, there is little doubt that racially the people were thoroughly mixed, as were all the inhabitants of the Greek peninsula since long before this date. As to language, we have a very intractable problem, because there is no really clear evidence for language from Macedonia until after the establishment of Greek as the common language of the eastern Mediterranean. In the time of Alexander, Macedonian could be regarded as a language separate from Greek, but such other indications that we have suggest that it was, nevertheless, a form of Greek, probably a very strongly differentiated dialect. One thing is clear, that well before the time of Philip and Alexander all the leading Macedonians were thoroughly at home in Greek. The religion of the Macedonians seems to have been entirely Greek, even if it had, as was normal, local peculiarities. In their culture and way of life, however, the Macedonians obviously did seem strange to the Greeks, and it was probably this, together with the language (or dialect), which led some of our Greek sources to call them *barbaroi* (non-Greeks).

The political arrangements were very primitive by Greek ideas. The king was the state; he controlled all internal and external policies. Not that he was a totally irresponsible autocrat; he had to be elected; for certain very important matters, like treason trials, a decision of the armed men was required; and he was expected to rule in accordance with the traditional laws. He governed through his Companions, the landed aristocrats to whom he gave great estates. They hunted, fought, and feasted by his side and had grown up with him through the institution of the Royal Pages, whereby the sons of the nobility lived with and served the king.

The potential strength of such a nation had never been realized because it was constantly under threat from its neighbors and subject to internal divisions. War was endemic among the peoples of the northern Balkans, who preyed on their neighbors almost as freely as they hunted animals, and the Macedonians shared the same customs. Within the extensive royal family there were frequent disputes about the succession, so that it was exceptional for the kingdom to be strong politically and united. In the reigns of Philip's father and his elder brothers, kings were expelled, assassinated, or dependent on the support of stronger foreign powers, like Thebes or Athens. Such a primitive and disunited state would hardly seem a probable threat to the great city-states of southern Greece.

Philip saw at close hand the treacherous and murderous intrigues within his own family, and came to power in a moment of desperate crisis, when his brother Perdiccas III had fallen, together with much of his army, in a disastrous defeat at the hands of the neighboring Illyrians, under their king Bardylis.

Multiple threats faced the new ruler: from the victorious Illyrians to the west; from the Paeonians to the north; and from at least two pretenders supported by foreign powers. Yet, within a year, all these problems had been managed in one way or another. In particular, he had trained his army so successfully that, in the summer of 358 B.C., he inflicted a crushing defeat on Bardylis and recovered the territories in western Macedonia previously lost to the Illyrians.

From then on Philip is virtually always campaigning and expanding. The main direction of expansion in the early years is eastward, toward Thrace. Here a number of Greek states stood in the way, and Athens, in particular, had important interests. In 357 B.C. he captured Amphipolis, the strategically placed city on the lower Strymon River, which was originally founded by Athens in 437 B.C., but lost in 424 B.C. and never recovered (even though the Athenians were never reconciled to that loss). It was characteristic of Philip's methods that he dissuaded the Athenians from helping Amphipolis by giving them to understand that he would hand the city over to them when he took it. Not only did he hold on to it himself, but he followed up his success by also taking Pydna, another city of interest to Athens. The most important of all his early conquests in this area, however, was of the Thasian colony called Daton or Crenides (which he refounded as Philippi) because that city controlled very rich gold mines. We are told that his annual income from these mines exceeded one thousand talents of silver, and from this time he always had abundant wealth to support his policies at home and abroad.

During the long and hard-fought struggle in central Greece known as the Third Sacred War, 355-346 B.C., Philip seized the opportunities it gave for expanding his power to the south. He became ruler of all Thessaly in 352 B.C., and by the Peace of Philocrates in 346 B.C. he obtained a dominating position on the Amphictyonic Council which controlled the Panhellenic Sanctuary of Delphi. Although he decided not to force the Pass of Thermopylae when he was opposed there in 352 B.C., the threat to his enemies further south, most notably to Athens, had been unmistakably demonstrated. During the same years he had continued to eliminate independent states close to Macedon, most strikingly the capture and destruction of Olynthus in 348 B.C., and he had begun his drive to the strategically important area of the Hellespont and Bosporus.

The Peace of Philocrates brought no true peace, and the opportunity for a final decision came through another dispute at Delphi, or so-called Sacred War, which Philip ended with his decisive victory over Athens, Thebes, and their allies at Chaeronea in 338 B.C. The control of all

Greece was the prize of this victory, and he established it very carefully by a mixture of military force and the subtle and complicated provisions of a peace treaty, the Treaty of Corinth, which ostensibly established general peace and autonomy throughout the Greek world.

In the spring of 336 B.C. as he prepared for even greater conquests his forces began the invasion of Asia Minor. How can we explain such extraordinary success? The basis was undoubtedly military. From the very beginning Philip devoted great attention to his army, training it in the most advanced skills and arming it with the most effective weapons. During his reign its size was dramatically increased. The infantry were about ten thousand strong at the beginning, with six hundred cavalry; by the end of his reign there were about thirty thousand foot and three thousand horse. This was the outstanding army with which Alexander conquered the Persian Empire. Unlike his more famous son, Philip was not invincible in battle. He suffered two severe defeats at the hands of the Phocians in 353 B.C.; he retreated from Thermopylae in 352 B.C.; he failed in his attempted sieges of Perinthus and Byzantium in 341-340 B.C.; and he did not necessarily totally destroy a defeated enemy. Demosthenes and many other Athenians were allowed to run away from the field of Chaeronea.

One reason for the slightly tarnished military record is that for Philip military glory was not a sufficient end in itself. If he could achieve his aims by other means he was glad to do so. It is clear, for example, that he employed bribery with great frequency and success, and the traitors whom he suborned were often instrumental in his successful destruction of their cities. He was also the supreme master of deception. He would hold off a potential enemy by friendship and promises until he was ready to turn against him. His victims were kept unaware of his true intentions until the last possible moment. The Olynthians, for instance, only realized at the very end that their city was to be destroyed and they were to be sold into slavery. In the protracted peace negotiations of 346 B.C. everyone was kept in the dark about Philip's intentions, until he had achieved the position from which he could dictate the terms that best suited his interests. He perceived his aims with complete clarity, and he was not hindered by any scruples in choosing the most effective methods to achieve them.

Does Philip reveal any weaknesses in politics and war? Many of the criticisms levelled at him in his own time seem misguided. One such concerned his extravagance: "When Philip came to be very rich," wrote Theopompus, "he did not spend his money quickly, he really hurled it and threw it away. He was quite hopeless at finance," (quoted by Hammond and Griffith 1979, 443). But generosity was a kingly quality, and Philip certainly used his wealth to gain his political ends. His large number of serious wounds in battle suggest to some that he exposed himself to danger irresponsibly. But here too he was performing to perfection the role expected of a Macedonian king whose leadership in war required that he fight intrepidly in the front ranks as the equal or superior of his men and Companions.

If there is irresponsibility in war, it appears more in a rather primitive pursuit of booty—though this too was doubtless necessary to keep the goodwill of his soldiers. When he returned from his Scythian campaign in 340-339 B.C., the army brought with it twenty thousand women and children captives, great flocks and herds, and twenty thousand well-bred mares. Not surprisingly, such booty impeded their military efficiency as well as tempting potential enemies. A powerful Thracian tribe, through whose territory they had to march, fell upon them. Philip himself was so badly wounded that he was for a moment taken for dead, and they lost all their precious booty. This was surely military irresponsibility.

Philip's notorious self-indulgence in his personal life also drew criticism from his Greek contemporaries. Here too we must distinguish what really concerned the political role of the king. Heavy drinking—the soldier's pleasure—was expected of Macedonian nobles and kings. That the king should satisfy his sexual desires without restraint was also generally expected in a system where even the Royal Pages were assumed to be available for the king's lust, should it take that direction. The polygamy practiced by the Macedonian kings is a different matter, because it affected the succession, always the most sensitive internal matter of all in a monarchical regime. Philip is known to have had seven wives. Nearly all of these unions seem to have resulted from the established custom of the Macedonians and their neighbors that agreements between states should be sealed by marriage alliances. Nevertheless, such polygamy inevitably leads to the bitter jealousies and intrigues about the succession which we think of as more characteristic of oriental kingdoms. In Philip's case, Olympias' son Alexander was early marked out to succeed, partly owing to his outstanding promise, partly perhaps also as a result of the unscrupulous deeds of his powerful mother. Alexander was given the best education the world could provide—Aristotle himself was his tutor, and positions of governmental and military responsibility were entrusted to him at very early ages.

It is little short of amazing, therefore, that in 337 B.C. Philip should have put his carefully constructed policy in jeopardy in order to indulge a middle-aged erotic passion. But his last marriage, to the young and noble Macedonian maiden Cleopatra, did just that. I see no reason to doubt the truth of the famous scene at the wedding banquet, which we know was reported by a contemporary source, Satyrus (Tronson 1984), even if the fullest account that we now possess is in Plutarch, a much later author.

> But before long the domestic strife that resulted from Philip's various marriages and love-affairs caused the quarrels which took place in the women's apartments to infect the whole kingdom, and led to bitter clashes and accusations between father and son. This breach was widened by Olympias, a woman of a jealous and vindictive temper, who incited Alexander to oppose his father. Their quarrel was brought to a head on the occasion of the wedding of Cleopatra, a girl with whom Philip had fallen in love and whom he had decided to

marry, although she was far too young for him. Cleopatra's uncle Attalus, who had drunk too much at the banquet, called upon the Macedonians to pray to the gods that the union of Philip and Cleopatra might bring forth a legitimate heir to the throne. Alexander flew into a rage at these words, shouted at him "Villain, do you take me for a bastard, then?" and hurled a drinking-cup at his head. At this Philip lurched to his feet, and drew his sword against his son, but fortunately for them both he was so overcome with drink and rage that he tripped and fell headlong. Alexander jeered at him and cried out, "Here is the man who was making ready to cross from Europe to Asia, and who cannot even cross from one table to another without losing his balance." After this drunken brawl Alexander took Olympias away and settled her in Epirus, while he himself went to live in Illyria. (Plutarch, *Life of Alexander*, 9.3-5, translated by Ian Scott-Kilvert, Penguin Classics. London, 1973)

Although a reconciliation was patched up later, it seems to me impossible to acquit Philip of dangerous irresponsibility about the succession. It is possible, but can never be proved, that he paid for it with his life. That the succession passed relatively smoothly to his son, after Philip was assassinated, was probably due more to Alexander's own ambition, competence, and ruthlessness than to anything Philip himself did in his disastrous last year.

There is, finally, the question of morality and public life. There cannot be any doubt that Philip was not a good man. The drunken revel among the enemy dead at Chaeronea is not a pleasant scene, and his repeated use of deception shows that he was not honest. But this is an old dilemma. In the ancient Greek world, as perhaps in all others, the sanctions of personal morality did not apply to dealings with foreign states, and even internally Macedonian public life was a dangerous jungle where cunning and ruthlessness were necessary for survival. Philip may have been morally reprehensible, but his achievements make him, by the standards of the world and of history, unquestionably great. He exemplifies perfectly Acton's sad dictum: "Almost all great men are bad men." Yet one of his most severe contemporary critics could say, "Never before had Europe produced such a man as Philip, son of Amyntas" (Theopompus, quoted by Hammond and Griffith 1979, 203).

# II

# Reconstructing the Skull of Philip of Macedon

*A.J.N.W. Prag*

LATE IN 1977 Professor Manolis Andronicos, himself a Macedonian, discovered what proved to be the first royal tomb in Macedonia while excavating the Great Tumulus in the village of Vergina, some forty miles west-southwest of Thessaloniki. To appreciate the full significance of his finds and of the identification of the occupant of the principal burial, it is important to understand the attitude of the Macedonians and the southern Greeks to each other, both in antiquity and in modern times. To the southerners, the Macedonians have seemed hardly to be Greeks at all, but the Macedonians themselves feel, and have long felt, that they are part of Greece—perhaps different from the people in the south, but certainly no worse. A discovery that could demonstrate to their advantage this cultural and racial unity was of great excitement to the Macedonians.

Toward the end of the fifth century B.C. King Archelaus moved the capital of Macedonia from Aigai to Pella. The identification of the site of Aigai had long been a problem in Macedonian history. Towns such as Edessa and Verroia had been proposed, without carrying much conviction, but recently Professor N.G.L. Hammond had, on good topographical grounds, suggested the village of Vergina (Hammond 1972, 156 ff.). A large Hellenistic palace had been known at Vergina since 1861, and the plain below the village is pockmarked with tombs, the majority from the Archaic period. No inscriptional evidence existed, but since the Macedonians continued burying their royal family at Aigai even after the move, the discovery of a royal tomb would provide conclusive proof. Elaborately built tombs of the fourth century B.C. had been found near the palace at Vergina, but all had been looted by ancient tomb-robbers. Thus, the unrobbed tomb (Tomb II), found along with two others under the Great Tumulus by Andronicos, might provide the key.

Tomb II was roofed with a semicircular barrel-vault. According to the traditional view, Greek architects learned how to construct such a vault only after Alexander the Great's campaigns in the East, which suggested a date for the tomb not much earlier than Alexander's death in 323 B.C. The point has been much debated; the most recent evidence suggests that barrel vaults were being built in Greece as early as about 350 B.C. In any case, the Vergina vault differs from the eastern, Mesopotamian examples because it is made with proper wedge-shaped stones, while Mesopotamian builders used squared bricks and filled the interstices with small stones. Further, Professor R.A. Tomlinson has argued most convincingly that the Macedonian builders experimented with the barrel-vaulting technique because they had a specific problem to solve created by their practice of burying notables in "heroic" tombs consisting of chambers concealed beneath tumuli, where the horizontal beams of traditional Greek architecture were impractical because they broke easily under the weight of earth above. By contrast, a vaulted arch spread the load to either side, while the side-walls themselves were supported because the whole structure was buried under a mound, thus overcoming one of the fundamental problems of stress in a free-standing arch (Tomlinson, 1987). Once one is prepared to accept the notion that at least by the second half of the fourth century the Macedonian court was not a cultural backwater, dependent for all inspiration on outside influences such as Athens or the civilizations of the East (as Demosthenes and the traditional "classical" view have had it), but was itself a source of innovation, then such a concept becomes much more feasible.

The tomb was unusual in that it had a main chamber, hastily completed, and an antechamber with much more carefully finished decoration; both contained a cremated burial. The bones had been carefully wrapped in a cloth of purple wool and gold thread, laid in a gold coffin or larnax decorated with a starburst (identified as the emblem of the royal house of Macedon), and placed inside a stone sarcophagus. The remains in the outer chamber have been identified as those of a young woman in her early or mid-twenties; those in the main chamber as belonging to a man aged between thirty-five and fifty-five. Found with the burials was a collection of magnificent objects including a silver-gilt "diadem" of adjustable size (probably indicating priestly rather than royal status: Andronicos 1984, 171-5, figs 138-9; but cf. Rolley 1987), a quantity of silver vases, a selection of armor and weapons, and the remains of a couch or bier decorated with miniature ivory heads. They have been described in detail by Professor Andronicos (e.g., Andronicos 1984, 119-97), and here it is enough to say that while the evidence of each item on its own can be disputed, taken all together the nature and quality of these finds suggest that the occupants of the tomb were members of the royal family. This becomes especially clear if one visits the marvelous new displays in the Archaeological Museum in Thessaloniki and contrasts the finds from this tomb with those from the other contemporary burials from Macedonia. Fine though the latter are, the sheer thickness of the silver and the quality of the craftsmanship of the Vergina metalwork puts it into a different league. The man was someone special.

Two finds from the main burial provide important clues to the date of the interment and the identity of the deceased. Four small black-glazed "salt-cellars" have been dated to the very end of the fourth century B.C., from parallels found in wells in the Athenian Agora. Yet more recent reconsideration of the finds from those wells show that some of the objects date from the third quarter of the fourth

century, so that the Vergina salt-cellars could date as early
as 340 B.C. (see Andronicos 1984, 221-224 for a summary of
the dating of the tombs).

The second object is a magnificent wreath of golden oak
twig found inside the larnax in the main burial. It is not
itself a symbol of royalty, but is the sort of wreath worn at a
banquet. Lovingly restored and complete save for a few
leaves and acorns, it is the heaviest and one of the two or
three most beautiful examples of such a wreath that we
have. The missing pieces were found at the site of the
cremation, on top of the tomb, swept up along with other
remains of the pyre when it was tidied up after the funeral.
Andronicos has argued that this demonstrates that the
deceased had been cremated on the spot immediately before
burial. He suggests a scenario where the dead man was laid
out on the pyre in all his finery, but as the flames began to
take hold, people tried to remove some of the best objects in
order to bury them with him rather than have them
destroyed by the fire. They were not quite fast enough with
the wreath, and it was touched by the heat so that a few
pieces fell off, to be recovered by the excavators 2,300 years
later (Andronicos 1984, 98-100, 171, 227, 232-3, fig 137).
Apart from its intrinsic interest, this point is important
when it comes to identifying the occupant of the tomb.

Accepting the tomb as a royal one of the second half of
the fourth century B.C. (and, incidentally, thereby confirming the identification of Vergina with Aigai), one has
only two serious candidates for the main chamber: Philip
II, assassinated at the age of 46 in 336 B.C. at Aigai on the
occasion of his daughter's wedding, or Philip II Arrhidaeus, half-brother and successor to Alexander the Great,
murdered by his step-mother Olympias in 317 B.C. when
he was 39 or 40 years old. (Alexander himself does not enter
the field, for he died in Babylon in 323 B.C. and was buried
in Alexandria.)

We know very little about the life or appearance of
Arrhidaeus. Although nominally king of Macedon for six
years, he seems to have been little more than a figurehead

for he suffered from some kind of physical and mental illness, used in turn by each of the generals fighting for supremacy in the years after Alexander's death. Plutarch tells us that his infirmity was not congenital, but that what had been a gifted mind was ruined by drugs administered by Olympias (Plutarch, *Life of Alexander*, 77.5; cf. Prag, Musgrave, and Neave 1984, 68-70, pl. V c-d). Although he is the favored candidate of those who prefer a date later in the fourth century for the tomb, there are several archaeological arguments against this theory. The most important is that he was not given royal burial until six months after his death, in 316 B.C., whereas, as we have seen, the evidence of the gold wreath shows that the deceased was cremated on the spot immediately before burial—something unlikely to have happened to a six-month-old corpse (Andronicos 1984, 227-8; for references to the disputed identification, Prag, Musgrave, and Neave 1984, n. 15; Green 1982, 129-51, gives a detailed analysis of the possibilities).

With Philip II the evidence is more compelling. His life story is reasonably well documented, and while we know little of his physical appearance from the ancient authors save that he wore a beard, they do provide some information on his extensive battle wounds. Further, a few possible ancient portraits of Philip II exist (I have brought these together elsewhere, see Prag, Neave, and Musgrave 1984, 70-77, pl. VI-VII; see also fig. 6). I have already argued that with little difficulty the tomb can be dated as early as 336 B.C., the year of his death, and Professor Andronicos has shown that the circumstances of the burial and of the tomb would fit (e.g. Andronicos 1984, 228-33). But even early in 1983, when his most recent summary was actually composed, Andronicos could do little more than argue from circumstantial evidence that Philip II was the most likely candidate, since no proof positive appeared to exist. Thus it was understandable that he should welcome what might appear to be a rather unconventional approach, a proposal to study the skeletal remains, in particular the skull, with a view to making a reconstruction of the dead man's appearance. The proposal came from an English team comprising Mr. R.A.H. Neave, Assistant Director of the Department of Medical Illustration at the University of Manchester, as medical illustrator, Dr. J.H. Musgrave, Senior Lecturer in the Department of Anatomy at the Medical School of the University of Bristol, as anatomist; and myself as archaeologist and coordinator. It is right that I should stress that the work that I describe here has been very much a joint undertaking, and that the credit for the exciting result achieved goes more to my two colleagues than to myself. And, of course, without Professor Andronicos' quite exceptional generosity in allowing us to study this unique material none of this would have happened at all.

Considering that we are dealing with a cremated body, the bones from the main burial in Tomb II at Vergina are in remarkable condition (fig. 1). Generally bones from ancient cremations, including the others from Vergina, are reduced to small fragments, but here we sometimes even have complete or near-complete bones (for example, the right ulna and the lower jaw), suggesting that the body was laid on some kind of platform to prevent its being shattered as the timbers of the pyre burned through and broke. This notion is confirmed by the presence of burnt clay bricks on the site of the pyre above the tomb (Andronicos 1984, 97-98; Prag, Neave, and Musgrave 1984, 77-78). From our point of view this was extremely fortunate, since otherwise there would have been little possibility of our achieving any useful results.

When one came to study the skull in detail, however, it was clear the work was not going to be straightforward. First, the top and back of the skull were distorted or missing, blown out during cremation, and had to be ignored. This in turn raised questions about the effect of the cremation on the form and size of the surviving fragments. Dr. Musgrave, therefore, carried out a number of practical tests, observing cremations of dry skulls carried out under laboratory conditions, from which he was able to conclude that although the skulls shrank by around 10 percent under the conditions of an ancient cremation, there was generally no distortion unless some extraneous factor intervened (Prag, Musgrave, Neave 1984, 61). This was important for Neave was having difficulty in fitting the casts of the surviving fragments of the skull together since they did indeed appear to be misshapen. This distortion could be detected on the upper jaw and cheek-bones but was most noticeable on the lower jaw, whose two ends are not level, while the midline of the teeth and the hollow in the center of the chin are pushed round to the "patient's" right by the distance of about two teeth (fig. 2).

Armed with the new information on the effects of cremation, Neave showed the bones to two facio-maxillary surgeons from the University Hospital of South Manchester, Mr. E. Curphey of the Facio-Maxillary Unit and Mr. John Lendrum of the Plastic Surgery Unit, both specialists in dealing with facial injuries and malformations. They concluded that we were dealing with a man who had a congenitally malformed face, underdeveloped on the left side and overdeveloped on the right to compensate; on the lower jaw this ability of the body to make up for such malformation was further shown by a natural remodeling of the chin, and by a thickening of the bone on the left side, presumably to give better anchorage for the muscles here, suggesting that our "patient's" ability to chew was in no way affected.

There was, however, no suggestion that his brain capacity need have been affected in any way (thus there was nothing here to connect him with Arrhidaeus' mental illness, even if we did not know that this had been brought on by drug addiction), nor even that it would have been particularly striking in everyday life. Very few people have a perfectly balanced face, and in antiquity there must have been many more mildly deformed people than there are today. Any museum collection of Greek terracotta figurines has its share of misshapen characters, not all of whom can have been intended as caricatures. Besides, in real life a beard such as the Macedonians habitually wore (until Alexander changed the style) covers many blemishes, so it need not surprise us that none of the Macedonian kings is credited with a twisted face by the contemporary writers (Prag, Musgrave, and Neave 1984, 66).

Having established the existence and the cause of these malformations, it became easier to fit the casts of the skull fragments together. Almost the first step in any reconstruction is to make accurate plaster casts of the skull or the skull fragments, using a mold made of dental algenate, which is flexible (and therefore safe to use on fragile bone) but gives a faithful impression. Such casts can be reproduced many times from a master, whereas the original bones, whether from an archaeological excavation or from a forensic case, are unique and irreplaceable. In the case of a damaged skull like the Vergina one it is then necessary to fit the casts of the fragments together, normally over a clay matrix which also fills in the missing areas (fig. 3); then a further cast is made of the "complete" restored skull, which provides the basis for further work. Where one is lucky enough to start with a complete skull, these intervening steps can be omitted.

The next step in the reconstruction depends on the realization that the form of any face is absolutely dictated by the shape of the skull beneath it; one may grow fatter or thinner, and of course one will grow older, but the basic shape and appearance of one's face will not change. The actual thickness of the flesh has been determined experimentally, most recently by a series of measurements made at twenty-one points over the skull by a team in New Mexico (Rhine and Moore 1982). To reconstruct the face, pegs are inserted into a cast of the skull to indicate the appropriate thickness at these twenty-one points, and the "flesh" is then built up muscle by muscle, following the strict rules of anatomy (and not artistic intuition), until the pegs are just concealed, then the whole can be covered with "subcutaneous tissue" and "skin" (fig. 4). The maximum size of the nose can be established by projecting the line of

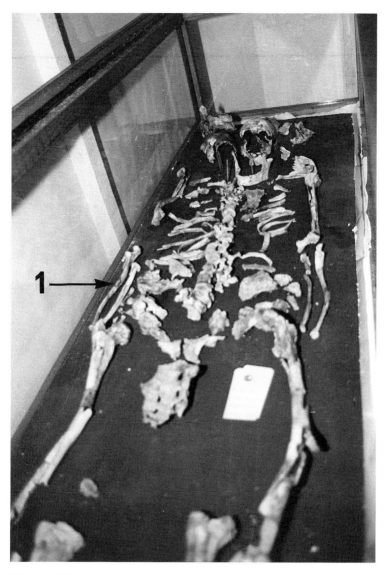

Fig. 1. The cremated skeleton from Vegina, Tomb II (main chamber): Philip II. 1: complete right ulna. From Thessalonike, Archaeological Museum. *Photograph by J.H. Musgrave, courtesy of Professor M. Andronicos.*

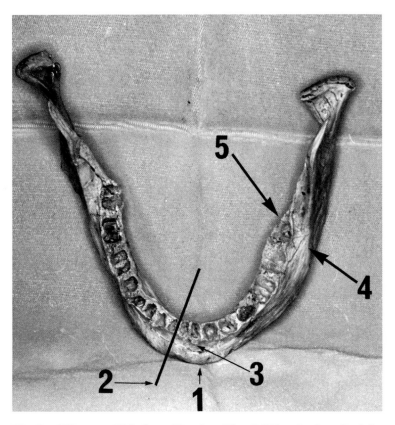

Fig. 2.   The mandible from Vergina, Tomb II (main chamber). 1,
3: remodelled chin; 2: dental midline, deviated to the right; 4, 5:
thickened bone, providing better muscle anchorage. From Thessalonike, Archaeological Museum. *Photograph by J.H. Musgrave, courtesy of Professor M. Andronicos.*

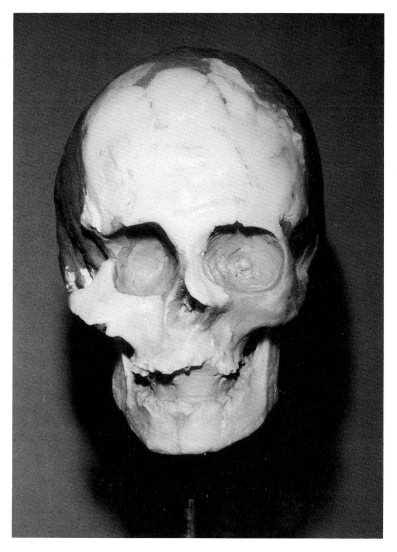

Fig. 3. The reconstructed skull from Vergina, Tomb II (main chamber): the white portions are casts taken from the surviving bones, the grey area is the clay matrix. *Photograph courtesy of the Department of Medical Illustration, University of Manchester.*

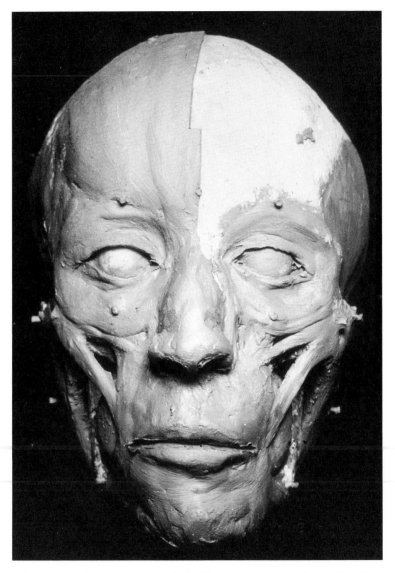

Fig. 4.   Partly reconstructed skull of a forensic subject, showing muscle and soft tissue built up over a cast of the skull. Some of the pegs indicated the thickness of flesh are still visible. *Photograph courtesy of the Department of Medical Illustration, University of Manchester.*

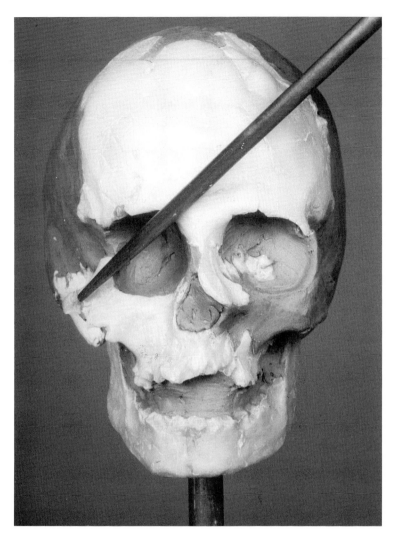

Fig. 5. The reconstructed skull from Vergina, Tomb II, showing the approximate course taken by the missile. *Photograph courtesy of the Department of Medical Illustration, University of Manchester.*

Fig. 6. Miniature ivory head of Philip II, from Vergina, with a nick in the right eyebrow suggestive of the injury. From Thessalonike, Archaeological Museum. *Photograph courtesy of Professor M. Andronicos.*

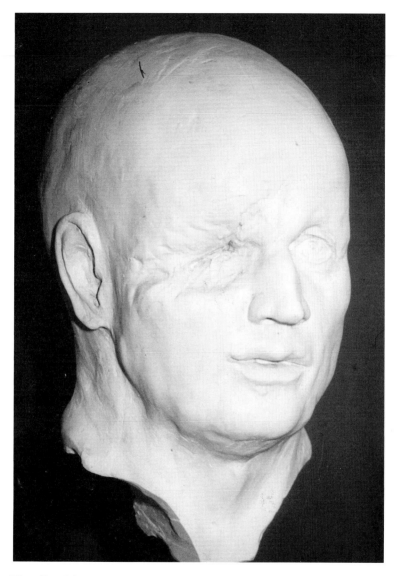

Fig. 7. Plaster cast of the reconstructed head of Philip II, showing the injury but lacking coloring and hair. *Photograph courtesy of the Department of Medical Illustration, University of Manchester.*

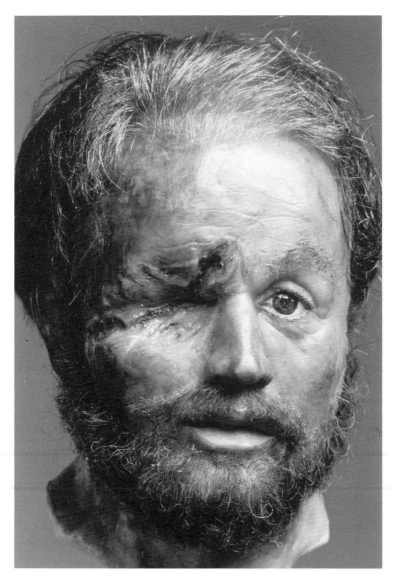

Fig. 8. Wax cast of the reconstructed head of Philip II, with hair, beard, and skin color. *Photograph courtesy of the Department of Medical Illustration, University of Manchester.* Note: the reconstruction of the wounded eye is not correct; see page 35.

the last third of the nasal bone downward, and that of the nasal floor outward, to give a triangle within which the nose must fit; because it is composed mainly of cartilage, one cannot tell the exact shape and size, but at least this projection gives the outer limits. Similarly, the width of the mouth is the same as the interpupillary distance of the eyes. (The process is described in detail in, e.g., Neave 1978, 168-78; Neave 1979, 149-57.)

The technique cannot produce a true portrait, which depends on all the wrinkles, minor blemishes, and quirks that give a face its individuality, as well as on an understanding of the "sitter's" character. That it can be used, however, to create an independent and accurate picture from a mere skull has been demonstrated not only by forensic reconstructions but also by controls performed under test conditions in the Medical School of the University of Manchester. Cadavers intended for dissection by students in the Department of Anatomy were photographed intact. After the dissections had been completed, the skulls were given to Neave, who then reconstructed their appearance, with no information other than their sex and age. When his reconstructions were compared with the photographs (which he had not seen before) the resemblance was uncannily accurate.

Thus we were confident, thanks to the highly specialized expertise that we could bring to bear on the remains, that a reconstruction based on the skull from Vergina would produce not only an accurate picture of the dead man, whoever he might be, but also reveal any surviving indication of illness or injury. Even though the study of the bones by Greek anthropologists had suggested that there was no evidence for either of these (Xirotiris and Langenscheidt 1981, 153, 158), our own specialist surgical colleagues had already detected congenital deformities of the face. We were not a little excited when they also found traces of damage to the inner upper corner of the right eye socket, and the marks of a healed fracture of the right cheekbone, which they explained as the result of a wound to the right eye which must have blinded it. On further consideration they defined this more specifically as a wound caused by a missile coming from above (figs. 3 and 5).

In the meantime, independently of their work (and without telling them of my own results so that they should not be influenced by them in any way), I had found evidence that Philip II not only was blinded in the right eye (this was common knowledge, for Demosthenes and several other authors list Philip's battle injuries), but also that, according to Didymus Chalcenterus, who wrote a commentary on the works of Demosthenes in the first century B.C., Philip "had his right eye cut out when he was struck by an arrow while inspecting the siege-engines and the protective sheds at the siege of Methone." In other words, he was injured from above, by someone shooting off the walls, in 354 B.C., eighteen years before his death (Didymus Chalcenterus, col. 12, 43 ff., on Demosthenes, *Philippic* 11.22; see Prag, Musgrave, and Neave 1984, 75-6 and esp. n. 38 for full references).

This was the confirming evidence that the man thirty-five and fifty-five year old man buried in the third quarter of the fourth century B.C. in Tomb II at Vergina must be none other than Philip II of Macedon; no other Macedonian king fits this combination of circumstances as well.

The facial reconstruction that was the next stage of our project turned out to resemble the supposed surviving ancient portraits of Philip II was interesting evidence but not itself crucial evidence. Some of these portraits seem to hint at the injury to the right eye. Most striking is the miniature ivory head, one of a series of royal portraits originally attached to a brier or couch placed in the tomb at Vergina (fig. 6). Above the right eye is a small nick, which Andronicos maintains is not the result of accidental damage to the ivory but was deliberately carved there by the artist to indicate the wound: even within the greater realism allowed in the so-called minor arts (to which this little piece belongs, for all its mastery), the conventions of Greek classical, idealizing art were still too strong to permit the depiction of this injury in its true horror. While this argument may well hold good, it is nonetheless worth noticing that the nick on the ivory is at the *outer* corner of the eye socket, whereas damage to the bone shows that the injury was to the inner corner.

In fact, the first state of our reconstruction (fig. 7), although it brought together all the crucial evidence in a convincing way, was not quite compelling (in the broadest sense of the word), for in lacking coloring and hair the head not only appeared rather lifeless but also resembled a much older man than the 46-year-old Philip. Therefore we called on the services of Ruth Quinn, a make-up artist with Granada Television in Manchester, who added the hair, beard, and coloring that were appropriate for a middle-aged, hard-living but probably well-nourished northern Mediterranean man: the king of Macedon, not as he would have appeared on his daughter's wedding day, the day of his assassination, but instead as he might have looked after a day's hunting. How to show the eye wound was a problem, but by one of those pieces of incredible serendipity with which this project has been favored, on the very day that she was working on the head of Philip, Ruth Quinn met a Canadian lumberjack who had suffered an almost identical injury some sixteen years before. Although it had not damaged his eye, it had left him with a badly scarred cheek because he was a long way from proper medical help. It was an easy matter to incorporate the evidence of his wound since at the time there was nothing to suggest that the Macedonian king had been able to have his appalling injury stitched, even properly cleaned (fig. 8).

The final result is an exciting and lifelike recreation of the king's probable appearance. This reconstruction is not and cannot be a portrait in the true sense of the word—indeed, we have already learned from a passage in Pliny that the rendering of the injury to the eye is inaccurate (*Natural Histories* 7.124. We owe this reference to Dr. Chrisotopher Ehrhardt). Philip's doctor, Kritoboulos, evidently won great fame for the way he extracted the arrow and healed the wound so that there was no scarring. We shall therefore have to make another version that lacks the gruesome scar, for display in the Archaeological Museum in Thessaloniki.

The congenital malformation can just be distinguished but as I have explained earlier, this would never have been very noticeable, and is further concealed by the beard. The case for Philip had been proved simply by the discovery of the injuries on the skull bones; all this extra work on the reconstruction took time and trouble. Yet it can be justified in a number of ways.

First, even Professor Andronicos did not apparently allow himself to accept the evidence of the injury until he had seen the reconstruction (and, later, had had the details pointed out to him on the casts of the bones themselves), even though he, and his team, were probably more familiar with the circumstances surrounding Philip's death and the evidence needed to link this skull with the king than anyone else. They, above all others, might have been expected to leap at the first shreds of evidence for the identification, yet even Andronicos never claimed in print that he had certainly found Philip of Macedon until then.

Second, not only the professional archaeologists found the reconstruction exciting and stimulating, and here I include not only the excavation team at Vergina but also those who heard our first presentation of these results at the International Congress of Classical Archaeologists in Athens in 1983, whether they immediately accepted our argument or not. As the newsstands in Athens testified the next morning, the reconstruction also captured and excited the imagination of the general public far beyond anything that a dry academic statement could ever do, and that surely is part of what the archaeologist's work is all about. For the modern Greeks it was clearly a marvelous moment to come face to face with that king of Macedon who had first united them, albeit reluctantly, after the battle of Chaeronea some twenty-three centuries before. In the identification of this rich tomb the Macedonians could see a justification of their claim to be part of the Greek nation, and (in their own eyes at least) a very special part of it.

# III

# Alexander in Egypt: Foundations for an Empire

*Murray C. McClellan*

ALEXANDER THE GREAT stands out from the pages of fourth century B.C. Greek and Macedonian history as one of those rare individuals whose leadership changed the course of the world. Like Caesar or Genghis Khan, Alexander led a well-developed military structure to dominance over a vast, multi-ethnic region. Like Lenin, Hitler, Mao, and many others, Alexander was the quite willing focus of a massive personality cult. Indeed, the multiplicity of stories that quickly developed about this enigmatic character have spawned numerous debates in the large body of scholarly work on Alexander.

While we can make an informed reconstruction of most events in the life of Alexander, we cannot fully fathom the intentions of this young Macedonian leader. We can be sure that Alexander had excellent intelligence on the Persian Empire he set out to conquer, and that he encouraged the creation of a new Greek and barbarian union in his kingdom. After Alexander's death in 323 B.C. and the subsequent division of his empire by his generals, this union proved to be illusory. The Macedonian/Greek culture formed an upper-class veneer over the old Persian Empire. The brilliance of the Hellenistic kingdoms that followed Alexander would have pleased him, though the son of Philip II could scarcely have foreseen the course they did take.

The best-documented example of the new political and social world resulting from the conquests of Alexander is

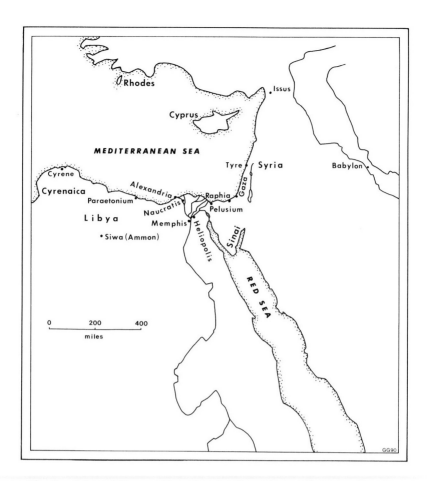

Fig. 1. Map of Egypt. *Drawing by Georgianna Grentzenberg.*

the Egyptian empire founded by the Companion of Alexander, Ptolemy Soter. In Alexandria, the first, and by far the most successful of the many cities that Alexander founded and named after himself, Greek poetry, art, and science thrived for several centuries (fig. 1). Our own lives would be vastly different if the culture that developed in Ptolemaic Egypt had never existed.

The story of Alexander in Egypt begins long before Alexander's arrival from Gaza in October 332 B.C. The Land of the Pharaohs was well known to the Aegean world of the Minoans and Mycenaeans (1800-1200 B.C.); throughout antiquity Egypt was one of the main grain exporters of the Mediterranean. Greeks first came to Egypt in significant numbers as mercenaries in the seventh century B.C., and, as tourists are wont to do, they left memorials of themselves in the graffiti that they wrote on monumental buildings (fig. 2). Close on the heels of the mercenaries were the traders. The Greek emporium (trading station) established in the Nile delta at Naucratis carried on important, though closely controlled, commerce between Greece and Egypt. Greeks were especially involved in Egyptian affairs during the reign of the pharaoh Amasis, before the conquest of the country by the Persian great king Cambyses in 525 B.C. (fig. 3). During the fifth century B.C. Greek scholars, such as Herodotus, visited Egypt and reported on its wonders. Following a revolt against the Persians that started in Cyprus in 380 B.C., the Athenian general Chabrias and the Spartan king Agesilaus commanded troops in Egypt used to support pharaohs who were independent of Persia. In 340 B.C., however, the Persian great king Artaxeres Ochus retook Egypt and held it until he was poisoned to death two years later. Thus, in 332 B.C., Alexander found an Egypt that had often turned to Greek-speaking soldiers to keep out the Persians. He took it without bloodshed.

Arrian, a second century A.D. writer who, by and large, provides the most trustworthy account of the life of Alexander, opens the third book of his Anabasis with the statement: "Alexander now set out for Egypt, his original goal, and marching from Gaza arrived after six days at Pelusium in Egypt" (3.1.1). It is clear that after Alexander defeated Darius at the battle of Issus in 333 B.C., the way to Egypt was open for the Macedonian leader. This prize was far more important than following immediately after Darius. Alexander besieged Tyre and Gaza and after making a difficult march through the Sinai, received Egypt from Mazakes, the Persian governor. Alexander, the Macedonian king, had closed the Mediterranean to the Persians. After wisely wintering in Egypt until the spring of 331

Fig. 2.    Graffiti on outer propylon at Karnak written by Greek and Carian mercenaries. *Photograph by author.*

Fig. 3. Quartzite head, thought to be of the Pharaoh Amasis. *The University Museum, Philadelphia, Inv. No. E.*

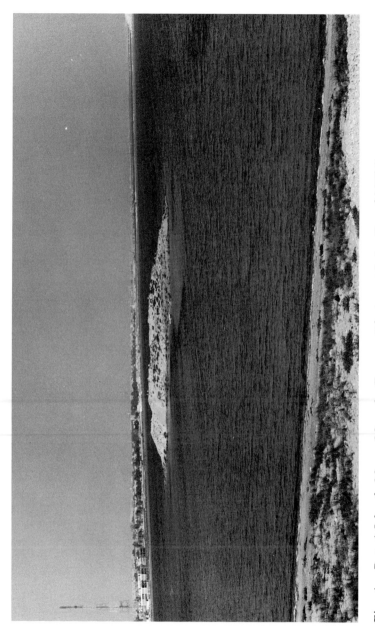

Fig. 4. Bates' Island, Marsa Matruh, Egypt. *Photograph by Donald White.*

B.C., Alexander began his eastern campaigns, and only returned to Egypt after he died, when his body was brought there from Babylon by Ptolemy Soter in 323 B.C.

Alexander began his brief trip to Egypt by going to Memphis, where he was hailed as pharaoh. Alexander no doubt won great popularity with the Egyptians by conducting proper, although purely Macedonian, sacrifices for the god Apis, a deity who had been scorned a few years before by the Persian Artaxerxes (Fraser 1972, 250).

Going no farther south than Memphis, Alexander went through the Nile delta and stopped at the Egyptian village of Rhacotis, opposite the island called Pharos, the future site of the greatest city of the Hellenistic world: Alexandria *ad Aegyptum*. Whether at this point in his trip Alexander founded the city that bears his name, or whether he did so after he returned from the Oracle of Ammon in the Siwa Oasis, has been debated by scholars (Welles 1962; Borza 1967; Bosworth 1988). In any case, as Arrian writes, Alexander was seized by a longing to visit Siwa.

The Macedonian army marched two hundred miles across the narrow coastal stretch from the western Nile delta and the harbor at ancient Paraitonium, identified with the modern Egyptian town of Marsa Matruh. In 1985, 1987, and 1989, The University Museum's excavations at Marsa Matruh, under the direction of Professor Donald White, were conducted on a small islet in a lagoon just east of the main harbor (fig. 4). Here, on the islet named Bates' Island after its discoverer, the excavators were rightly rewarded in their search for evidence of Late Bronze Age (1600-1200 B.C.) trade between the Aegean, Cyprus, and eastern Libya. The number and variety of foreign, especially Cypriot, pottery types that were found in late fourteenth century B.C. contexts bear witness to an active trade with the Eastern Mediterranean.

Of equal historical importance was the evidence that was found for the occupation of Marsa Matruh in the sixth and third centuries B.C. (White 1986, 1989). Bates' Island yielded traces of substantial structures of these periods. The

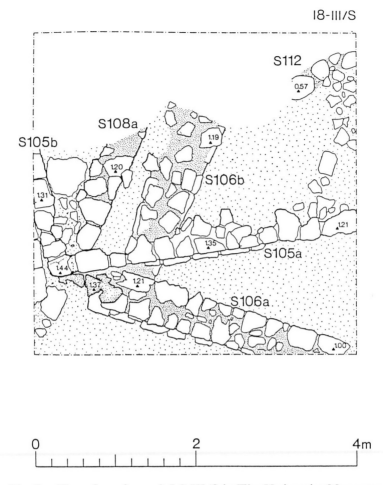

0              2              4m

Fig. 5.   Top plan of trench I-8-III/S in The University Museum 1985 excavations at Marsa Matruh. Two structures of the third century B.C., S106 and S108, are overlaid by the walls of a later Roman structure, S105. *Drawing by J. Thorn and C. Beetz.*

associated pottery clearly shows that the harbor of Marsa Matruh was utilized by Greek traders as early as the late sixth century B.C. It would seem that by the end of the third century B.C. the harbor was regularly used by traders who plied between Egypt and the northern Mediterranean (fig. 5.).

It is certain that the well-established Greek colonies to the east in Cyrenaica were active in this trade. The people of Cyrene worshipped a combination of Zeus and the god of the oracle at Siwa, Ammon. Other ancient sources for Alexander's trip to Egypt, Diodorus Siculus and Quintus Curtius, relate that a gift of three hundred horses, sent by Cyrene to Alexander, arrived in Paraitonium. That the deified Alexander of the Hellenistic Age continued to be important in Cyrene is documented by the discovery of a small limestone head of Alexander which had been de-dicated in the Extramural Sanctuary of Demeter and Persephone (fig. 6). This statuette head found in The University Museum's 1976 season of excavations in Libya (also directed by Donald White) is a local, and not terribly successful, adaptation of the type that shows the *pothos* of Alexander, with its head uplifted to heaven. The remarkable small ivory head found by Andronikos in the Great Tomb at Vergina demonstrates that this type originated in the fourth century and is thus not a product of a mixed, baroque Greek and Eastern style of the later Hellenistic period (Bieber 1964, 63-67).

It is outside the scope of this paper to discuss the religious significance of Alexander's trip to Siwa (Welles 1962; Bosworth 1977). Suffice it to say that later generations believed Alexander had been addressed by the priests of the oracle as the son of the god. Alexander took a small force with him for the perilous trip through the desert; he planned to use small springs between Marsa Matruh and Siwa to supplement the supplies which would not last the entire eight-day journey (Engels 1978). The Macedonians were in serious trouble when they encountered a sand storm along the way. There is no reason to doubt the tradition that Alexander was led to the oasis by the flight of birds headed in that direction.

There is some evidence that Alexander consulted the oracle about the foundation of the city of Alexandria (Borza 1967; but cf. Fraser 1972, 247). In any case, we should doubt the statement by Ptolemy Soter, written after he had established his kingship in Egypt, that Alexander made the extremely hazardous 330-mile trip directly from Siwa to

Memphis. We would certainly have heard from other sources if Alexander had managed a desert trek that had swallowed up part of Cambyses' Persian army in 525 B.C.—Alexander no doubt returned to Paraitonium on his way out of Egypt after Siwa.

Alexander spent the winter of 332/331 B.C. in Egypt. He visited Memphis, the future site of Alexandria, Marsa Matruh, and Siwa. He left Egypt under the governorship of Cleomenes, and for the rest of his brief life, Alexander directed his attention to the east. It is inconceivable, however, that he did not appreciate the wealth and the potential represented by Egypt, and that he did not plan to return to the Nile at some time. In any case, Alexander's conquests marked a new age for Egypt. The Greek-peaking military had become a ruling class that was to dominate the country for centuries. Such a major cultural shock was not felt again in Egypt until its conquest by the followers of Mohammed.

The empire that Ptolemy was able to wrest from the other claimants to Alexander's legacy originally encompassed much more than the Nile Valley, although Egypt was always the center of the Ptolemaic kingdom. During the third and second centuries B.C., the Hellenistic kingdom of Egypt became a pawn in the civil strife of the growing world power—Rome. Three centuries of Ptolemaic rule had transformed Egypt into a new, multi-ethnic entity. This new Egypt, home of Greek, Jew, and native Egyptian, was to survive basically intact throughout the rule of the emperors of Rome and Constantinople. For a millennium, the hub of this transformed Graeco-Roman Egypt was the city Alexandria. That Alexander was personally involved with the foundation of Alexandria is not questioned. The story, however, that Alexander laid out the course of the future city using barley-meal shows what an ephemerial role the king had in its construction. The initial Greek building of Alexandria was carried out by Deinocrates of Rhodes in the period when Alexander was in the east and Cleomenes ruled from Memphis. In 323

Fig. 6. Limestone head of Alexander from The University Museum excavations at the Sanctuary of Demeter, Cyrene, Libya. *Photograph by Donald White.*

B.C., Ptolemy Soter tricked the other Macedonian generals by bringing the body of Alexander to Egypt instead of transporting it back to Vergina. Ptolemy quickly seized power in Egypt; he was able to move his capital, and the corpse of Alexander, from Memphis to Alexandria within three years.

Alexandria was ideally situated for its purpose—to be the major trading port of the Eastern Mediterranean and the seat of an imperial power that was to dominate the Greek world in the third century B.C. (fig. 7). As a first century A.D. visitor, Strabo remarked, Alexandria was laid out in the shape of a riding cape on the stretch of land between Lake Mariotis and the sea. In an engineering feat that was first used in the siege of Tyre, the island of Pharos was joined to the mainland by an artificial causeway (the Heptastadium) that created two good harbors. Along the eastern harbor was built the famous Museum and Library of Alexandria. The city was laid out according to an orthagonal, or Hippodamian plan, a few scant traces of which have been found in rescue excavations.

Our main evidence for early Alexandria comes from the cemeteries, such as the one at Chatby, which may contain burials of the first generation of settlers. The material remains from early Alexandrian tombs are, not surprisingly, closely matched by those from contemporary Macedonia. The architecture and painting styles would be quite at home in Macedonian Veroia or Lefkadia. A pebble mosaic floor from a house that was built at Chatby after the area ceased to be a necropolis shows close affinities to one from the Macedonian capital of Pella. The Macedonian taste for beautiful mosaics was quickly adopted in Alexandria.

The early painted stelai (grave stones) from Chatby present an idealized portrait of the ruling class of Greeks and Macedonians and remind us that Alexandria was always *ad Aegyptum*, or on Egypt, and never a part of the old Egypt of the pharaohs. While this ruling class allowed the native Egyptians to adopt the old iconography of

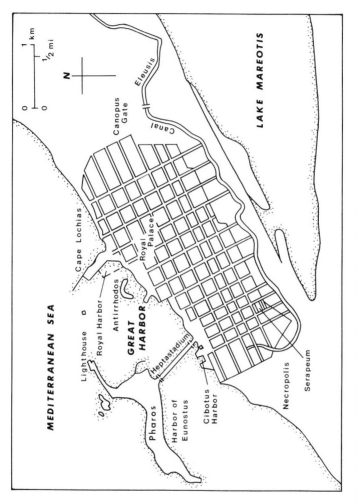

Fig. 7. Map of Hellenistic Alexandria. *Drawing by Georgianna Grentzenberg, after A. Aymard and J. Auboyer, L'Orient et la Grèce antique, (Paris, 6th ed., 1967), p. 442.*

Fig. 8.   The Fort of Mohammed Bey at Alexandria, the site of the Pharos Lighthouse. *Photograph by author.*

pharaonic Egypt to portray the new Greek regime, the Greeks continued to represent themselves in a purely Greek manner.

Alexandria, whose population was to reach one million, was a city of architectural marvels. The Lighthouse of Alexandria, built on the island of Pharos, was one of the famed seven wonders of the ancient world (fig. 8). As later copies show, the tower was tripartite, with square base, hexagonal middle, and round tip. The Lighthouse was topped by a large statue and a fire beacon, and it could be seen by sailors miles away at sea. The palace complex of the Ptolemies, which contained the famous Museum, the Library, and the Sema—the tomb of Alexander and Ptolemy Soter—may now lie under water (Frazer 1972, 23). The lure of Alexander's tomb has sparked many wild attempts to find it, although it is known that the tomb was partially looted by later Ptolemies. While the discovery of the Sema would cause a sensation, it would not yield the sort of riches recently uncovered in the royal Macedonian cemetery at Vergina (Andronicos 1984).

The approximate location of the Ptolemaic palace of Alexandria is given by the former position of the famous Cleopatra's Needles, two obelisks brought to Alexandria from Heliopolis by Augustus to adorn the new Caesareum or Temple of Augustus. Augustus also transported Egyptian obelisks back to Rome, incorporating one as the gnomon of a massive sundial near his Ara Pacis. The engineering challenge of moving colossal obelisks has had a lasting appeal to imperial powers. Egyptian obelisks can be found in Istanbul and in Paris, and Cleopatra's Needles were shipped to London and New York in the 1870s.

Alexandria was a city of contrasts. Its fountains and its horticultural and zoological gardens offered relief from the busy pace of a commercial city. Its streets, echoing to the babble of many languages, were a fertile ground for new ideas. The new spirit of Alexandria can best be seen in its most important religious compound—the famous Serapeium, where a new, synthesized deity, Serapis, was worshipped along with his more popular consort, Isis (Rowe 1946).

The Ptolemaic dynasty proved to be exceptionally powerful and long-lasting. Each Ptolemy and his queen ruled over a court that was to attract the most intelligent minds of the age. Alexandria was the queen of the arts, the home of the poetry of Theocritus and Apollonius, the literary criticism of Zenodotus and Callimachus, and the scientific investigations of Aristarchus and Eratosthenes. The visual arts flourished, in both large-scale work and delightful miniatures.

The Ptolemies used Egypt as their personal estate from which they could draw resources to conduct imperialistic policies in the Mediterranean. Cyprus, the Cyrenaica, and the Aegean at one time or another were all Ptolemaic foreign possessions (Bagnall 1976). Ptolemaic foreign policy was directed to keeping its possessions and to warding off the other Hellenistic kingdoms. In the late 260s B.C. Ptolemy II, Philadelphus, supported the Athenians in their revolt during the Chremonidean War and constructed a fort at Koroni in Attica. The late third century saw a series of battles between Ptolemy IV, Philopator, and Ptolemy VI, Philometer, and the Syrian king Antiochus the Great (III) and Antiochus Epiphanes (IV). At the battle of Raphia in 217 B.C., Ptolemy Philopator was able to maintain his control over southern Syria by arming twenty thousand native Egyptians. In a few years, however, the Egyptian army was defeated at Banias, a site now in northern Israel, and Antiochus Epiphanes was only prevented from seizing Egypt through the intervention of Rome. As a consequence of the new-found power of the native Egyptians, later Ptolemies, such as the boy-king Ptolemy V, were forced into giving concessions to the original occupants of the Nile Valley.

We should end by examining one curious aspect of the ancient economy of Ptolemaic Egypt. There is no doubt that the Ptolemaic kingdom was a great producer of both agricultural and manufactured products. There are massive

Fig. 9.   Encaustic mummy portrait. *The University Museum,*
*Philadelphia, Inv. No. E16214.*

amounts of records that show the tight control exercised by the crown in the economic affairs of the country, especially in matters that concerned the royal monopolies (Préaux 1939). It has often been commented on, however, that the technological discoveries, such as Archimmedes' screw, made by the creative Hellenistic intelligentsia were never applied to the realities of improving the productivity of the country. While discoveries, such as the elaborate astrological mechanism from a first century B.C. shipwreck off Antikythera in southern Greece, show that in fact practical applications of Hellenistic science were made, it is true that little attention was given by the Greek kings of Egypt to increase production; unlike all modern economists who see an increase in the rates of production as a social good, ancient economic planners strove to maintain equilibrium (Samuel 1983). The produce that was given by the annual flooding of the Nile was duly collected, but no attempt was made to try to squeeze out more than the traditional methods yielded. All was directed to maintaining the status quo.

Eventually, however, the sought-after equilibrium was to crumble. During the course of the last century B.C., the class of slaves and urban proletariat grew enormously. Dynastic struggles rocked Alexandria and fierce race riots broke out all over Egypt. Recently, the focus of Ptolemaic scholarship has shifted from examination of the large body of Greek texts to examination of the equally large number of papyri written in the Demotic of the native Egyptians (Bagnall 1982). We can now see that native Egyptians were little affected by the Greek dynasty. The real admixture of Egyptian and Graeco-Roman, as illustrated by the well-known Roman mummy portraits (fig. 9), did not occur until after the suicide of Cleopatra, when Egypt became the possession of the first Roman emperor, Augustus.

The Nile River, a giver of life, had nourished an Egyptian culture that continued essentially unchanged for more than twenty-five centuries until the beginning of the first millennium B.C. In 331 B.C. the Macedonian army took control of those riches, and for the next one thousand years the ruling class in Egypt spoke Greek. Such was the legacy of Alexander.

# IV

# Philip of Macedon, Alexander the Great, and the Ancient Olympic Games

*David Gilman Romano*

A LIMITED BUT IMPORTANT aspect of the lives of Philip of Macedon and Alexander the Great was their interest in competitive athletics in Greece, and specifically, their relationship to Olympia and to the ancient Olympic Games. Olympia was a rural sanctuary of Zeus in the western Peloponnesos (fig. 1) that was the site of a religious festival which became one of the most famous festivals of ancient Greece. Olympia was named in antiquity after Mount Olympos, the highest mountain in mainland Greece, located on the border between Macedonia and Thessaly. In Greek mythology, Mount Olympos was the home of Zeus, the leader of the pantheon of Greek gods and goddesses. From at least 776 B.C. the religious festival of Zeus at Olympia included athletics, and these contests were the most well known of antiquity.

Athletes would come to Olympia from all over the Greek world which then included not only mainland Greece, but also Greek colonial cities from distant regions of the Mediterranean and as far north and east as the shores of the Black Sea. The athletes who came to compete at Olympia shared many characteristics: they were all male citizens of Greek city-states, they all spoke Greek, and they all held the same religious and cultural beliefs. They came every four years to Olympia in late summer and celebrated a festival in honor of Zeus that included dedications and sacrifices as well as athletics.

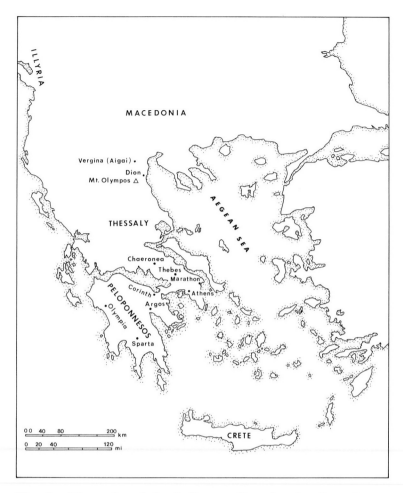

Fig. 1. Map of mainland Greece. *Drawing by Georgianna Grentzenberg.*

Macedonian interest in the ancient Olympic Games is known as early as ca. 500 B.C. when Alexander I, son of Amyntas (who would become king of Macedonia 498-454 B.C.) and an ancestor of Philip of Macedon, competed at Olympia in the *stadion* race, a foot race one length of the stadium. The Macedonians had been regarded by the Greeks as being on the fringes of Greek civilization, and Herodotus, the fifth-century historian, explains how Alexander I was not allowed to compete until he had proven his Greek descent to the officials at Olympia.

> For when Alexander chose to compete [at Olympia] and entered the lists for that purpose, the Greeks who were to run against him were for barring him from the race, saying the contest should be for Greeks and not for foreigners; but Alexander proving himself to be an Argive, he was judged to be a Greek, so he competed in the *stadion* race and ran a dead heat for first place. (Herodotus *History* 5.22)

Some have called into question the validity of this story since Alexander I's name does not appear in the victors' list from Olympia (Roos 1985, 163-167). It is known for certain that approximately one hundred years later in 408 B.C., Archelaus, another Macedonian king, son of Perdiccas, won victory at Olympia in the *tethrippon*, the four-horse chariot race (Moretti 1957, 110-11).

In 359 B.C., Philip II, as a young man of 23, became the ruler of Macedon. It is known that shortly thereafter in 356 B.C. he won the first of three equestrian victories at Olympia in the *keles* (horse race). Philip commemorated his victory by issuing silver coinage in several denominations with the image of Olympian Zeus on the obverse and a victorious horse and jockey on the reverse. The jockey is naked and is holding a palm branch and wearing a victor's fillet on his head. The inscription reads ΦΙΛΙΠΠΟΥ (of Philip). An example of one of Philip's silver coins, a tetradrachm, is illustrated here as figure 2. Philip would also win chariot victories at Olympia (in either the two-horse chariot *synoris*, or four-horse chariot *tethrippon* in 352 and 348 B.C. (Moretti 1957, 124). It may be that his victory in the two-horse chariot race at Olympia was the reason the issue of a series of gold staters (see fig. 3) showing the head of the youthful Apollo on the obverse and a two-horse chariot with charioteer on the reverse. The same inscription, ΦΙΛΙΠΠΟΥ (of Philip), is found below

Fig. 2. Silver tetradrachm; Obverse: head of Zeus; Reverse: horse and jockey with inscription, ΠΙΛΙΠΠΟΥ, ca. 356 B.C. The University Museum, no. 29-126-58. *Photograph by the author.*

Fig. 3. Gold stater; Obverse: head of Apollo; Reverse: two horse chariot with inscription, ΠΙΛΙΠΠΟΥ, ca. 350 B.C. The University Museum, no. 29-126-59. *Photograph by the author.*

the chariot. Although Philip won these three impressive victories in the Olympic Games, it is interesting to learn that he was neither the jockey nor the charioteer on any of these occasions, nor was he even at the site of the contests! For by the fourth century it was not unusual for the owner of a horse to employ a jockey or charioteer as well as the other necessary personnel to take care of all the various needs of equestrian competition.

Plutarch, a first-century A.D. Roman author, gives us this account of Philip's learning of his first Olympic victory in 356 B.C.

> To Philip, however, who had just taken Potidaea, there came three messages at the same time: the first that Parmenio had conquered the Illyrians in a great battle, the second that his race-horse had won a victory in the Olympic Games, while the third announced the birth of Alexander. These things delighted him, of course, and the seers raised his spirits still higher by declaring that the son whose birth coincided with three victories would always be victorious. (Plutarch *Life of Alexander* 3.4-5)

In about this same time, or shortly thereafter, Philip founded new Olympic festivals in Macedonia at Aigai and at Dion, modelled on the Peloponnesian festival, although Diodorus (17.16. 3-4) attributes the founding of the Olympic Games at Dion to Archelaus.

At the time of the three victories at Olympia, Philip was king of Macedonia and a military and political leader of growing importance in the Greek world. Philip became even more important to the Greeks in 338 B.C. when he and his well-trained Macedonian army fought the combined forces of the allied Greek army at Chaeronea, near Thebes, in Boeotia and won a decisive victory. As a direct result of this battle, Philip became the leader of all the Greek city-states; he immediately assembled the allied Greek forces at Corinth and united them with a plan to liberate the Greeks of Asia and to conquer once and for all the Persian Empire.

One of Philip's most conspicuous acts following the battle was to commission the building of a lavish structure at Olympia in the heart of the most sacred aspect of the sanctuary of Zeus, the *altis*. It is not known whether or not Philip visited Olympia to pick out the site for the building, but it seems very likely that he would have. The area selected had previously been reserved for the buildings and shrines in honor of gods and heroes—Zeus, Hera, and Pelops (one of the mythological founders of the Olympic Games) among them (fig. 4). The new building that Philip commissioned was circular, with an exterior colonnade of eighteen Ionic columns and an interior colonnade of nine engaged Corinthian columns. Pausanias, a second century A.D. traveller, gives us this description for the building (fig. 5).

In the Altis is a round building called the Philippeion. On the roof of the Philippeion is a bronze poppy which binds the beams together. The bulding is on the left of the exit over against the Prytaneion. It is made of burnt brick and is surrounded by columns. It was built by Philip after the fall of Greece at Chaeronea. Here are set statues of Philip and Alexander, and with them is Amyntas, Philip's father. These works too are by Leochares, and are of ivory and gold, as are the statues of Olympias and Eurydice. (Pausanias 5.20.9)

The name of the building, Philippeion, meant literally "Philip's building," for its purpose was not to bring honor to Zeus or Hera or Pelops, but instead to commemorate Philip and his family. In Greek architecture, round buildings were still fairly unusual at this time as was the combination of the exterior Ionic and the interior Corinthian orders; it has been suggested that the architect of the building came from Macedonia (Miller 1973, 189). The location of the building itself must have brought it great attention and it undoubtedly served as a physical symbol of

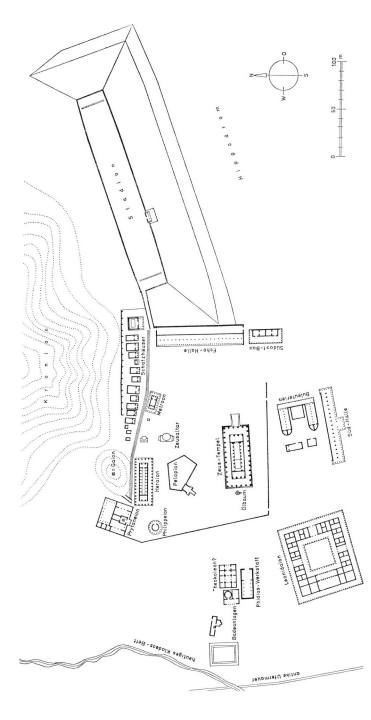

Fig. 4. Plan of Olympia, fourth century B.C. *Reprinted from Herrmann 1972, 162.*

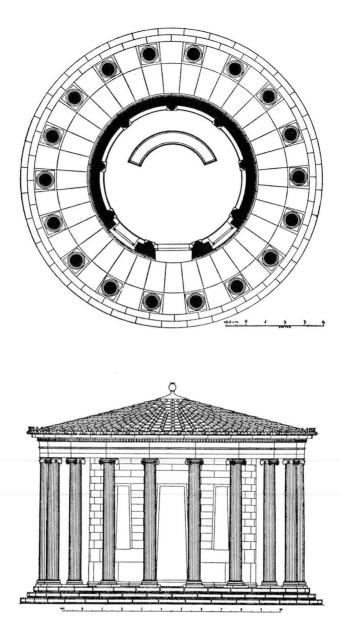

Fig. 5. Philippeion ca. 336-333 B.C. Top: ground plan;
bottom: elevation. *Reprinted from Hermann 1972, 171.*

Philip's undisputed supremacy over the Greek states (fig. 6). In fact, Philip considered himself to be descended from Herakles, as did all Macedonian kings. According to Pausanias, Herakles was the founder of the Olympic Games as well as a great grandson of Pelops (Pausanias 5.13.2). It is possible that Philip located his monument close to that of Pelops to emphasize this relationship (Miller 1973, 192).

As Pausanias describes above, gold and ivory statues (a medium normally reserved for cult statues) of Philip and his family by the sculptor Leochares adorned the interior spaces of the building. Leochares was one of the premier sculptors of the fourth century B.C. who, at that time, had already distinguished himself as one of the four sculptors who had worked on the Mausoleion of Halikarnassos. The Mausoleion would later be included in the lists of the seven wonders of the ancient world.

When Philip was assassinated in 336 B.C., the construction of the building was likely to have been incomplete, and it is most probable that Alexander, Philip's son and successor, at the time only 20 years old, oversaw the completion of the structure.

It is generally agreed that Alexander was physically strong and muscular—what would be termed athletic in the modern day. It is interesting to learn, however, that he never competed in the Olympic Games. Plutarch recounts a number of anecdotes about Alexander that have some bearing on this point.

> Being nimble and swift of foot, he was urged by his father to run in the stadion race at the Olympic games. "Yes, I would run," said he, "if I were to have kings as competitors." (Plutarch *Moralia* 179.2)

Plutarch also tells another story about Alexander that may help to explain the first.

When Krison, the famous *stadion* runner raced Alex-

Fig. 6. British Museum model of the Sanctury of Zeus at Olympia as it would have appeared in the Hellenistic period (ca. 200 B.C.). This view is from the west and the Philippeion is located in the middle ground (left). Immediately behind it is the Temple of Hera, to the near right is the Pelops shrine, and to the far right, the Temple of Zeus. *British Museum Photograph.*

ander and appeared to slacken his pace deliberately, Alexander was very indignant. (Plutarch *Moralia* 471.E.F)

Although Alexander did not compete in the Olympic Games, he did come to associate himself with Olympia in a number of ways, both during his lifetime and after his death. Alexander appears to have continued the Macedonian Olympic Games at Aigai and Dion, adding contests in poetry and music and wild beast shows (Plutarch *Life of Alexander* 4.6). But perhaps Alexander's greatest contribution to the spread of athletics and the ancient Olympic Games was both a direct and indirect result of his eastern campaigns which took him through Asia Minor, Egypt, Mesopotamia, and Persia to Bactria and India. Very literally, Alexander and his army brought Hellenic culture as well as Greek physical training and competition to the corners of the then known world.

From an account of Athenaeus, a second century A.D. author, we learn that two of Alexander's most trusted and valuable military officers, Perdiccas and Kraterus, were both athletes and lovers of physical training. They were known to have brought with them on their extended military campaigns a good deal of athletic paraphernalia.

> Perdiccas and Kraterus, who were lovers of gymnastic activities, always had in their train piles of goat-skins as big as a *stadion*, under cover of which, after appropriating a place in the encampments, they would carry on their training; they were also followed by a long train of animals carrying sand to be used in the palaistra. (Althenaeus 12.539)

One would have to imagine that a full-scale portable gymnasium and palaistra would be set up in the army's encampment. The goatskins would likely have been used as a roof to provide shade for the training athletes to simulate a stoa, *xystos*, six hundred feet long for the runners. There would also have been an enclosed court, palaistra, including sand, for the practice of wrestling, boxing, *pankration*, and other types of physical exercise. Perdiccas and Kraterus would not have been the only users of the portable gymnasium, other officers and soldiers would have trained as well. For it is known that Alexander routinely held athletic and musical contests for his troops after military victories and on other successful occasions in his eastern campaign. For example, contests were held at Susa, Persepolis, Ecbatana, and Taxila. According to the second century A.D. author Arrian (7.14.10) the funeral for Alexander's friend Hephastion included athletic and musical contests for three thousand.

Proof that Alexander had great respect for athletes and especially Olympic victors is found in Arrian (2.15), who reports that Alexander restored liberty to Dionysidorus of Thebes, who had been taken prisoner at the battle of Issus in 333 B.C., because he was an Olympic victor.

Strabo, a first century A.D. geographer, mentions in the *Geography* (15.1.67) that as soon as Alexander's army entered India, the native craftsmen turned in great numbers to the production of strigils and oil containers, both necessities for athletic training.

Alexander's influence can be easily appreciated by the following account by the author of the *Maccabees* of the second century B.C. who reports that young priests in Jerusalem were neglecting their temple responsibilities in order to practice throwing the discus.

Philostratus, a second century A.D. author, describes the physical arrangements for the training of a local Indian ruler. The facilities were clearly influenced by Greek standards.

> The bathing place was a garden, a *stadion* in length, in the middle of which was dug out a pool, which was fed by fountains of water, cold and drinkable; and on each side of the pool there were race courses in which he was accustomed to practice after the manner of the Greeks with javelin and discus.

To return again to the Sanctuary of Zeus at Olympia, it must be said that Alexander realized the great importance of the religious site especially when he was thousands of miles away in the eastern territories. It is known, for instance, that he published at Olympia the records of his various military successes in the east. In 324 B.C. he sent Nicanor to read before the Olympic festival crowd the order for all Greek cities to recall their exiles (Diodorus 18.8.2-5).

From the German excavations at Olympia, as well as from Pausanias (6.16.5), comes evidence for a specific monument which has been found in the southwest corner of the Sanctuary of Zeus (fig. 6). It is the remains of a statue base of limestone which carries an inscription (fig. 7) that reads:

> King Alexander's courier and surveyor of Asia, son of Zoites, a Cretan from Chersonesus, dedicated this to Olympian Zeus.

The Greek word for courier is *hemerodromos*, which means, literally, "day runner." Perhaps the most famous day runner from Greek history was Pheidippides, who brought news to Sparta of the Persian invasion at Marathon in 490 B.C. The Greek word for surveyor really meant "route measurer" or "stepper." Whereas a day runner was technically not an athlete in the sense of competing, he certainly would had been a very fit long-distance runner. On the same base where the inscription is found it is very likely that there was attached a bronze tablet that would have included a map of the surveyed areas of Asia that Philonides had stepped out, the territories conquered by Alexander (Dittenberger and Purgold 1896, 403-4).

Although Alexander died of a fever in Babylon in 323 B.C. at the young age of 33 years, because of his conquests new Hellenistic athletic festivals were established in many of the cities of the Hellenized East, including Alexandria, Antioch, Ascalon, Damascus, Gaza, Laodicaea, Perge, Tarsus, and Tyre to give only a partial list. Many of the athletic contests of these festivals were set up on the model

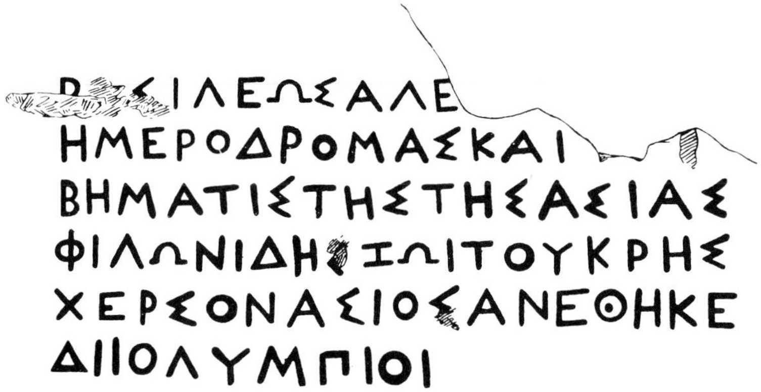

Fig. 7. Philonedes inscription from Olympia, ca. 325 B.C.
*Reprinted from Dittenberger and Purgold 1896, 402-4.*

of the Olympic Games and were called *isolympian* meaning, literally, "equal to the Olympic Games" in regu-
lations, honors, prizes, and probably in other ways as well.
We know, therefore, that in each one of these cities
gymnasia, palaistrai, as well as stadia and hippodromes
would have been constructed and athletes would have
trained and competed in the Greek manner. Throughout
the Hellenistic period, many of these athletes from North
Africa, Asia Minor, Asia, and the Levant came to compete
at Olympia.

It is interesting to note that even after Alexander's death
his associations with Olympia continued. On a famous
series of coins issued from various cities of the Hellenized
East (see figs. 8a and 8b), Herakles is shown wearing the
lionskin on the obverse; some have seen this head as a
portrait of Alexander himself. On the reverse side of the
coins, the seated Olympian Zeus is depicted with the
inscription ΒΑΣΙΛΕΩΣ ΑΛΕΞΑΝΔΡΟΥ (King Alexander).
Zeus holds an eagle in his right hand and a sceptor in his
left hand, showing a marked similarity to the image of the
colossal gold and ivory cult statue of Zeus in the Temple of
Zeus at Olympia (Kraay 1966, 349).

A

B

Fig. 8. Silver tetradrachm; **A** Obverse: Herakles wearing the lion skin; **B** Reverse: Olympian Zeus seated on a throne holding eagle and scepter with inscription, ΒΑΣΙΛΕΩΣ ΑΛΕΞΑΝΔΡΟΥ, after 232 B.C. The University Museum no. 29-126-63. *Photograph by the author.*

## Philip of Macedon, Alexander the Great, and the Ancient Olympic Games

Philip of Macedon and Alexander the Great spent very little time at Olympia, but it may be said that they had a great and lasting influence at the Sanctuary of Zeus as well as on the ancient Olympic Games and generally on the conduct and spread of Greek athletics. Largely because of foreign campaigns they spread Greek culture, including language, art, religion, and architecture along with physical training and athletics, to the lands of the East. Philip and Alexander also understood well the religious, social, and political importance of Olympia, and used it to their fullest in order to promote their goal for the unity and the supremacy of the Greek states.

# V

# Religion in the Age of Philip II, Alexander the Great, and Their Successors

*Irene Bald Romano*

OUR KNOWLEDGE OF the culture and religion of
the Macedonian people in the period predating the fourth
century, that is, the period of Philip II and Alexander the
Great is largely limited to what can be gleaned from
archaeology in that region and from Greek and Latin
written sources. Archaeology tells us plenty about burial
customs but little about the cults, cult practices, and native
gods and goddesses of the Macedonian people. When our
Greek sources begin to describe their northern neighbors,
we learn that well before the age of Philip and Alexander,
the Macedonians were looking to the Greek pantheon and
to Greek religious customs, and that they were using Greek
myth to legitimize their dynastic claims. When as early as
the seventh century B.C. the town of Aigai was adopted by
the Macedonians as their capital, the choice was blessed by
an oracular response of the Pythian priestess at Delphi, the
most sacred and widely recognized Greek oracular sanctuary (Hammond 1972, 433-35). And in 476 B.C. Alexander
I, a forbearer of Alexander the Great, to qualify for admis-
sion in the Olympic Games, laid claim to a royal genealogy
going back six generations to the most Greek of Greek
hero-gods, Herakles (Badian 1982, 34-35).

Although there were "Philhellenes" among the prede-
cessors of Philip II, whether for political expediency or
because of a true admiration of Greek culture (Badian 1982,
36-37), in the reign of Philip II (359-336 B.C.) the Macedonian claim to "Hellenism" was most convincingly and

consistently stated. The gods of Philip II were those of the Greek pantheon. He was rewarded by Apollo with seats on the Delphic Amphictyonic Council after his victory in the Sacred War in the mid-fourth century B.C., and he participated, *in absentia*, in the games sacred to Zeus at Olympia by virtue of his claim to descent from the family of Herakles. Philip built his own family monument in the heart of the sanctuary at Olympia—a dedication to his beloved Zeus and an ostentatious display of political power and religious fervor (fig. 1).

The court of Philip II was a mixture of Greeks and Macedonians; his son, Alexander, became the physical embodiment of his conscious policy of integrating Greek and Macedonian culture. Alexander's tutelage at the feet of the Greek philosopher Aristotle is well documented. His knowledge and love of the Greek poets and the Homeric heroes is also well documented though much exaggerated and romanticized in our contemporary historical novels (Badian 1982, 39-40).

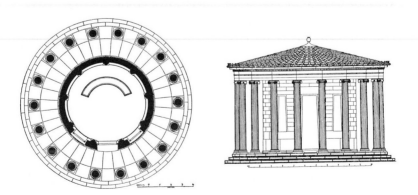

Fig. 1.  Plan and reconstruction of Philippeion in the Sanctuary of Zeus at Olympia. Ground plan after *Ol. Forsch.* 1, pl. 2; reconstruction by H. Schleif (*Ol. Forsch.* 1, Altas, pl. 1). *Reprinted from H.-V. Herrmann, 1972, p. 171, figs. 121-22.*

By the mid-fourth century B.C., as far as we are able to determine, Macedonian culture in general was essentially Greek in character, but probably retained a specifically Macedonian ethnicity. There is no doubt that by this period the religion of the Macedonians, at least of the ruling and upper classes, was essentially Greek. But in Macedonia, as in Greece proper, there were local divinities and cults and a local flavor to festivals and worship. We know that Zeus the Highest was the chief god of the Macedonians, and that Herakles in his various aspects was given special veneration. We also know of the existence of certain local Macedonian festivals and the deities they celebrated, but it is difficult to extract detailed information about Macedonian cult activities (Hammond and Griffith 1979, 149, 164-5).

Macedonian history and art in the age of Philip and Alexander attest to the essentially Olympian character of the religion of the ruling and upper classes. The iconography of the Macedonian royal house was eclectic but infused with Greek mythology. Alexander the Great affirmed his ancestral bond with Herakles by adopting the head of Herakles wearing the skin of the Nemean lion—the symbol of one of Herakles' successful labors—as the portrait on the obverse of his coins (fig. 2A). Alexander continued to harp on this link with Herakles, and through his life and deeds he presented himself as the historical Herakles hero (Pollitt 1986, 25-26).

Allusions to Zeus are also common in Macedonian royal iconography from the age of Philip and Alexander. A seated Zeus, holding an eagle and scepter, is the reverse image on the coins of Alexander (fig. 2B). The head of Zeus is the obverse image on the coins of Philip. This choice is a reference to Philip's Olympian victories and his ancestral links to the supreme ruler of the gods and the father of Herakles (fig. 2C). After Alexander's visit to the oracle at Siwa in the Libyan desert, he adopted for his portrait an image of himself wearing the horns of Zeus Ammon on coins minted in Alexandria.

A               B

C               D

0     2

cm

Fig. 2. **A**: Obverse of silver coin of Alexander the Great minted in Amphipolis (ca. 324-323 B.C.). The University Museum, Philadelphia, Acc. No. 29-126-62. **B**: Reverse of silver coin of Alexander the Great minted in Babylonia (329-336 B.C.). The University Museum, Philadelphia, Acc. No. 29-126-469. **C**: Obverse of silver coin of Philip II minted in Macedonia (359-336 B.C.). The University Museum, Philadelphia, Acc. No. 29-126-58. **D**: Obverse of gold coin of Arsinöe II minted in Alexandria (ca. 181-145 B.C.). The University Museum, Philadelphia, Acc. No. 29-126-546. *Photographs by The University Museum Photographic Studio.*

The recently excavated tombs at Vergina have provided us with a wealth of spectacular painted representations to illustrate still further the Greekness of the mythology of the Macedonian upper classes. In one tomb is a daring composition of Pluto's rape of Persephone with Pluto on his four-horse chariot grasping Persephone. Hermes runs in front of the chariot while a frightened companion crouches at the back (see *The Search for Alexander* 1980, 26-31, esp. 30, fig. 13).

The cult of Dionysos also had great appeal among the Macedonian people in the fourth century B.C., and in general throughout Greece in the succeeding centuries. The most spectacular evidence is the three-foot high bronze krater found in a relatively modest grave at Derveni, just north of Thessalonike in Macedonia. Although some experts argue that the krater is of South Italian, Corinthian or Attic origin, it can be demonstrated that the workmanship and iconography indicate at least a Macedonian sponsorship for the manufacture of this unique piece, created around 340-330 B.C. (Barr-Sharrar 1982, 133-34). The scenes on the krater recreate the life of Dionysos: the youthful Dionysos relaxing with his leg draped over Ariadne's leg, and Maenads and Silens, attendants of Dionysos, dancing in a state of ecstacy on either side. Four separately cast figures adorn the shoulders of the krater: Dionysos, a sleeping Maenad, a tipsy Satyr, and another Maenad. (See the photographic details in *The Search for Alexander* 1980 pls. 20-21 and figs. on pp. 164-65).

With the conquests of Alexander and the rapid expansion of Greeks and Macedonians into new lands came the strong impact of the cultural values of non-Greek peoples on Greek culture. New forms of religious beliefs and the worship of new gods profoundly influenced Greek religion in the period following Alexander. Contributing to the influx of new religious ideas in this period was the breakdown of the stable foundations on which Greek society and traditional religious ideas were based. First, the dissolution of the *polis* or city-state, the political unit which provided a framework for the Greek citizen, led to feelings of alienation and isolation that caused Greeks to look for new religious values to answer their needs. Second, the rise of the ruler-cult suggesting that man should no longer look to the gods of Olympos alone for guidance and punishment, but to a mortal ruler who required the veneration once due only to the gods. Alexander increasingly assumed autocratic power, declaring himself king and reinforcing his power with claims to divinity. Even before his death, divine cults of Alexander were founded (Walbank 1982, 41-43, 213). The successors of Alexander who ruled the carved-up portions of his empire continued to foster the notion of the ruler-cult, none perhaps with more success than the Ptolemies of Egypt (Walbank 1982, 213-18) (fig. 2D). The founding of cities, sanctuaries, and festivals in their honor and the naming of tribes and calendrical months after them established a pattern that was followed in many of the Hellenistic kingdoms. The obvious effect of the establishment in Greek lands of the worship of divine rulers was a growing skepticism toward the traditional Greek gods.

This Hellenistic period, from the death of Alexander in 323 B.C. to the break-up of the last Hellenistic kingdom in the first century B.C., is known as the age of syncretism in Greek religion (Grant 1953, xiii-xx). It is in this period that Greeks allowed foreign gods into their pantheon and foreign cult practices into Greek cities and shrines, amalgamating traditional Greek gods with non-Greek ones to create new deities to worship. In Ptolemaic Egypt, for example, the traditional gods of Egypt continued to be worshipped after Graeco-Macedonian control was established, but the cult of a fabricated Graeco-Egyptian god, Serapis or Sarapis, was much cultivated (fig. 3). This new god embodied elements of the Egyptian Osiris and the Apis-bull, as well as of Zeus, Hades, and Asclepius. Serapis was an underworld deity who was able to heal the sick and perform miracles. The Ptolemies' motive in fostering the cult of Serapis was to furnish a god whom the native

Fig. 3. Marble statues of Isis and Serapis from Gortyn, Crete
(Roman Period). Archaeological Museum of Heraklion, 260, 259.
*Reprinted from R. Salditt-Trappmann, Tempel der Ägyptischen
head Gütter in Griechenland und an der Westkste
Kleinasiens, (Leiden: E.J. Brill, 1970), fig 48.*

Egyptians could worship in common with Greek settlers. We are told by ancient sources that a Greek sculptor, Bryaxis, was commissioned by one of the Ptolemies to create the look of this new god, although which Ptolemy and when exactly this image was made is problematic (Pollitt 1986, 279-80; Austin 1981, 438-40 no. 261). Serapis is usually shown in sculptural representations bearded and seated wearing a chiton and himation with a kalathos or basket on his head, and holding a staff or scepter and cornucopia. Sometimes the figure of Kerberos, the three-headed dog of the underworld, is shown with him. The cult of Serapis was especially popular in Egypt in the third and second centuries B.C. and spread from there to East Greece, the islands, and Italy.

The cult of Serapis, however, never achieved the wide-spread and sustained appeal that the cult of another Egyptian deity, Isis, did in the Hellenistic and Roman periods (fig. 3). Isis was in Egyptian mythology the sister and consort of Osiris, the divine king, and the mother of Horus. She was a popular figure, yet there was no great veneration of her as distinct from the rest of the Egyptian gods until the Hellenistic period when a cult of hers was founded in Alexandria. From the cosmopolitan port of Alexandria the cult spread around the Mediterranean, especially to other port towns and commercial centers. It made its way to Sicily and Italy and was firmly entrenched there by the early decades of the first century B.C. In Roman times the cult of Isis was very strong among the masses despite attempts by various rulers to suppress it, since these shrines of Isis were looked upon as centers of subversive activity and licentiousness (Witt 1971).

Part of the appeal of the cult of Isis in the Hellenistic period seems to have been its mysterious nature (fig. 4). Devotees believed that there were certain mysteries that could be revealed only to those initiated through special ceremonies. As in most mystery cults, members believed that through these ceremonies the initiated could commune with their beloved deity and could achieve salvation

Fig. 4. Wall painting of Ceremony of Isis Cult from Herculaneum, Italy (1st c. B.C.). Transferred to panel in Museo Nazionale, Naples. *Reprinted from T. Kraus, Pompeii and Herculaneum: The Living Cities of the Dead, (New York: H.N. Abrams, 1975), fig 256. Photograph by L. von Matt.*

or some esoteric wisdom. Most of what we know about the activities of the cult of Isis, we have learned through authors of the post-Hellenistic period, such as Apuleius, who in the second century A.D. wrote his famous *Metamorphoses,* popularly known as *The Golden Ass.* This work in part records the initiation of the hero Lucius into the cult of Isis (11.1-25). Apuleius describes Lucius' preparations, up to the suspenseful moment of his initiation, and the epiphany of Isis with her flowing hair garlanded with flowers, wearing her tunic of many colors, and carrying a bronze sistrum and a golden cup. Apuleius breaks off the description to tell us in Lucius' words: "I would tell you [what went on] if it were lawful for me to tell, and you would know all if it were lawful for me to tell, and you would know all if it were lawful for you to hear." He breaks off again and says he can only tell us :

> I drew near to the confines of death, treading the very threshold of Proserpine. I was borne through all the elements and returned to earth again. At the dead of night, I saw the sun shining brightly. I approached the gods above and the gods below, and worshipped them face to face. See, I have told you things which, though you have heard them, you still must know nothing about. I will therefore relate only as much as may, without committing a sin, be imparted to the under-standing of the uninitiate. (Grant 1953, 136-44)

Mystery cults in general had tremendous mass appeal in the Hellenistic period (see Burkert 1987). We can attribute the popularity of the cult of Dionysos, for example, to its orgiastic mystery elements. These mystery cults may well have depended on wine, drugs, or hypnosis to induce the desired end—a pleasurable feeling of final enlightenment in the devotee. The predominance of healing cults and the belief in miracles is also tied in this period to this interest in mystery or salvation cults.

Worship of an eastern deity, Kybele, an Anatolian mother-goddess whose homeland was supposed by the Greeks to have been Phrygia in central Turkey, was already in place in Greece in the sixth century B.C., but her appeal was much heightened in the Hellenistic period and con-tinued to spread in the Roman period. Again, the appeal of this cult rested on its mysterious nature, the feeling in the initiated of belonging to a special group to whom salvation was granted. Attractions to joining the fold were, no doubt, the flamboyant and grotesque rites—flagellation and castra-tion of the priests of the cult and loud hypnotic playing of

cymbals that accompanied colorful processions of devotees
dancing in ecstasy or collecting alms (Vermaseren 1977).
Cult images of Kybele depict her, in contrast to the wild
nature of her rites, as a conservative deity seated regally
with the emblems of her cult, usually the lion (a reference
to her origins as the Tamer of Lions, the Mistress of the
Wild Animals), a cymbal or tympanum, the musical instru-
ment used to assist in the frenzied state of the participants
in the cult, and a phiale or libation vessel (fig. 5).

Interest in other foreign, especially Near Eastern, cults
was also very strong in this period. The cult of the Syrian
fertility goddess, Artargatis, for example, was especially
popular in parts of the Hellenistic east (Grant 1953, 116-
22), and so too was the mystery cult of Mithras, an ancient
Indo-Iranian god of light and truth, which gained even
greater popularity in the Roman period (Ferguson 1970,
47-49).

Also during this period, especially in the Hellenistic
East, Asia Minor and Egypt, members of the Persian
priestly caste called Magoi cultivated astrology, practiced
secret rites, and gave special veneration to the sun god,
Helios, and to Zoroaster, the semi-divine inventor of magic
(Grant 1953, 112-16). Indeed, it was from these Magoi,
people whom the Greeks thought practiced magic, that the
Greeks began to use the word *magos* or *magoi* for magi-
cians. The renewed interest in magic and the occult during
the Hellenistic period exemplifies the search by the common man for answers no longer found in traditional
religious beliefs. It was in this period that astrology,
alchemy, and daemonology were combined in a system of
applied science that was taught, probably mostly in secret,
under masters of the occult (Luck 1985, 6, 14-15, 25-26).

Information on these subjects is supplied to us in ancient
poetic texts, handbooks, treatises on very technical subjects,
and recipes and formulas for everyday use. From the
Magical Papyrus in Paris we have a recipe for a love potent
that would send sleepless nights to a young woman with
whom a young man was in love:

Fig. 5. Terracotta statuette of Kybele from Gordion, Turkey
(late 3d to early 2d c. B.C.). In Archaeological Museum of
Gordion. Gordion excavation no. 2152 T35. *Photograph courtesy
of Gordion Excavation Archives, neg. 71642.*

Fig. 6. Marble statue of Tyche of Antioch. Roman copy of
original by Eutychides (ca. 295 B.C.). In Vatican Museum.
*Reprinted from J. Onians, Art and Thought in the Hellenistic
Age, (London: Thames and Hudson, 1979), p. 99, fig. 101.*

Take the eye of a bat and release it alive. Take unbaked dough made from wheat flour or wax that has not burned, and shape a puppy dog. Put the right eye of the bat into the right eye of the puppy and the left eye of the bat into the left eye of the puppy. Take a needle and stick the magic substance onto it ...

The formula continues with other instructions and some mumbo-jumbo, and finally,

Make [the chosen young woman] be sleepless because of love of me forever and ever. (Luck 1985, 101)

Beyond this, widespread belief in superstition was cultivated. In this period, formulaic sayings, lucky numbers, and amulets with powers were grasped with renewed vigor. Lead curse tablets on which a suspected enemy could be named and damned in some way were also particularly frequent from this period (Luck 1985, 18-20).

Greeks also turned increasingly in the Hellenistic period to the worship of abstractions, especially to the goddess Tyche or Chance or Fortune (fig. 6). This, in itself, is symptomatic of this age when the Greek world had broken out beyond all traditional boundaries, geographically, scientifically, and philosophically, into utterly new and imaginative places and fields of inquiry. This was an age, probably not unlike our own in some ways, in which Greeks were forced to search for direction and meaning no longer directly imposed on them by the bounds of city, custom, or religion. In some ways, Tyche or Fortune was a comfortable diety to worship for she could take life out of the hands of mortals and move circumstances, for good or bad, in a divine way. Man, in her hands, was not responsible for his fate—his destiny was predetermined. But Tyche was also a deity to fear, for according to Menander, "Fortune observes no rules by which she decides human affairs" (Frag 355K) (Pollitt 1986, 1-3).

So, it was in magic, superstition, and personalized mystery religions that Greek people of the Hellenistic period sought refuge from a world which probably seemed to be out of control. The Hellenistic Age, initiated by Philip II and Alexander the Great of Macedonia, was a deeply religious and thoughtful age, but a time when traditional Greek religion took second place to scientific inquiry, to philosophic questioning of religious beliefs, and to the syncretism of Greek religious ideas with foreign or personal beliefs.

# VI

# Alexander in India: The Last Great Battle

*Gregory L. Possehl*

$I$T IS COMMONLY CONCEDED that Alexander the Great of Macedon was perhaps the world's greatest military genius. His conquests reached from Greece to the borders of the Ganges Valley in India, a march of over three thousand miles from the west to the east, taken as a linear measurement. With his conquest of Egypt in the south, a detour to subdue to Sogdians in Central Asia, and a circuitous route of actual march, the journey was much longer than this. I have not laid out what we know of the actual route, but it was certainly twice the direct distance (fig. 1).

In 336 B.C., one year after the assassination of his father, Philip II, Alexander assembled an army that he intended to use in a conquest of Persia, at that time the most powerful political and military force in Asia and Europe. We are told that the force he mustered consisted of only thirty thousand infantry and forty-five hundred cavalry (McCrindle 1896, 17; cf. Tarn 1948, 10). This pursuit was in fact something that Alexander inherited. The Greeks and the Persians were long-time enemies. Philip II had led Greeks against the Persians during his life; thus, it was probably only natural that Alexander carry on.

Alexander's genius for military strategy and tactics, his charismatic leadership, and the strength and bravery of the men in his army proved to be too much for his enemies. First Anatolia, then Egypt and Mesopotamia, and finally Persia and its capitals of Susa and Persepolis fell to the

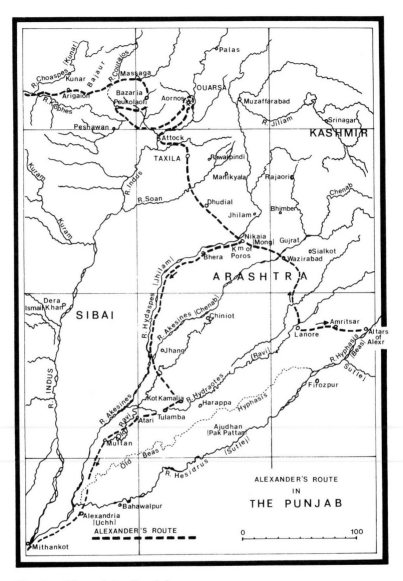

Fig. 1.   Map of the Punjab.

youthful Macedonian and his army. It is an impressive story, and one that is surprisingly well documented, given the fact that it began some 2325 years ago.

The best and most complete story of Alexander's adult life was compiled by Arrian, a Greek historian of the second century A.D.[1] It is both a story of Alexander's campaigns and a description of ancient India. Arrian's book is a rich source of information on the Indian campaign and the inhabitants of that "distant" land—distant as far as the Greeks were concerned. I have taken this account of Alexander's time in ancient India, plus my own observations as a sometime traveler in the Punjab, to form this story of Alexander's last great battle.

Following Alexander's conquest of the Persians, he travelled further east to Bactria where he subdued the remaining elements of the Persian army. Then, to secure his northern flank he moved into what we now know as Central Asia and defeated an ancient people known as the Sogdians; there he took a wife, Roxana.

This brings us to February 326 B.C., when he crossed the Indus River just above Attock, very close to the place where the Indus and Kabul Rivers join. This river crossing marks his formal entry into ancient India, now part of the modern nation-state of Pakistan.

Alexander's reputation might have preceded him to India, which best explains the warm welcome he received from Taxiles, governor of the ancient city of Taxila, just west of the modern capital of Pakistan, Islamabad. At Taxila, Alexander apparently learned that a king named Porus, a powerful ruler of western India, intended to oppose his further advance to the East. So, after an interlude which included a Greek sacrifice and an athletic contest, his army marched east to the Hydaspes River (the modern Jhelum) accompanied by Taxiles, other Indian governors, and a contingent of an additional five thousand

---

[1]   His book has been translated by P.A. Brunt under the title *History of Alexander and Indica*.

Indian troops. They were preceded by a flotilla of boats, including large thirty-oared craft, which Alexander had ordered transported over land to the Hydaspes. These craft apparently had formed the bridge use by the army to cross the Indus River.

Arrian (Brunt 1983, 2:29-31) tells us that Porus was observed across the river, which was swollen and running fast and deep—an indication that it was at least early spring. Another reference suggests it was the May solstice, when the Himalayan snow melt brings the rivers of the Punjab back to life. It is apparent that Alexander was in no particular hurry to make a direct amphibious assault across the river, into a force whose military ability was untested and whose size and composition were imperfectly known, if known at all. We know only that Porus' squadron of war elephants had been sighted. Given these unknowns, and the dangers inherent in an amphibious assault, Alexander undertook a ruse. For weeks he busied his troops by sending them along his side of the river in mobile deployments. His flotilla sailed here and there. The cavalry were kept on the move, drawing the attention of Porus first in one direction and then another. Alexander at one point even announced that he would wait until winter before attempting a crossing, so that he could take advantage of the lower, less turbulent river conditions, as well as the cooler weather. He clearly understood the value of rumors and was confident that Porus had his own network of spies to bring him his news.

When it was estimated that Porus had become complacent, Alexander decided to make a secret crossing. He had learned something about the local landscape (but not enough, as we shall soon see) and had found a well-wooded place where the river turned. The turn was so great and the ground cover on both sides sufficiently dense that it would have been very difficult for Porus to observe a crossing made in its vicinity.

To provide a mask for his crossing Alexander began once again his deception. This time it was a short-term maneuver aimed at first at arousing Porus' interest and alertness, and then at lulling his adversary into a sense that all was routine and that his vigilance was still being played with. The resulting shifting of troops, clatter of armor, and howls of the Greek war cry had their intended effect. Porus followed the initial forays with appropriately intense attention, which then slackened as he saw that all the activity fit into the larger pattern of the earlier days and weeks. It is somewhat ironic that this part of Alexander's plan allowed him to make the real preparations for his invasion across the Hydaspes out in the open. And so he did, covered in addition by the fact that it rained the night before the planned river crossing.

Leaving a detachment in reserve, with detailed orders about their possible engagement in the forthcoming battle, Alexander and his infantry, javelin throwers, archers, and cavalry made the crossing the following morning. They were immediately spotted by outliers of Porus' army, who scurried away to inform their king. Alexander soon found to his surprise and dismay that he had not actually crossed the full river. Instead, he had landed on an island, a large island to be sure, and another dangerous water crossing lay ahead—even the greatest military leaders have erred.

Alexander must have known that his battle plans were now vulnerable and that he had to act with speed and decisiveness if he were to succeed. Thus, the search for a ford was made immediately, and one was quickly found. It was shallow enough for the infantry to cross on foot, and the horses could swim. There are some differences among the ancient sources on what happened after they crossed from the island to the farther bank of the river. Arrian recounts (Brunt 1983, 2:43-54) that some say there was a battle at the landing led by Porus' son, in which Alexander was wounded and his favorite horse, Bucephalas, was killed. Others indicate that Alexander sent his cavalry against these forces and inflicted heavy damage on them, killing Porus' son. At any rate, all agree that Alexander eventually made it across both the island and the adjacent river and that both Bucephalas and Porus' son died during this battle on the Hydaspes.

Having made the second crossing, Alexander and his cavalry and mounted archers led the way to Porus' forces. The infantry made a forced march behind them.

Arrian (Brunt 1983, 2:47) tells us that Porus had wisely selected the field of battle in an area with firm sandy soil—a location which would support his chariots and give firm footing to his animals and men. He had fielded about four thousand cavalry, three hundred chariots, two hundred elephants and thirty thousand infantry. They had been disposed in the following way. He put his elephants in the center and forward, each separated by about one hundred feet. If Arrian is correct, the elephants alone would have been a battle line over three and one half miles long. Filling the gaps between the elephants, but slightly behind them, were infantry units. Additional infantry formed the flanks beyond each side of the line of elephants. The flanks of the infantry were protected by cavalry fronted by chariots. This was a formidable battle array. The elephants and infantry were tightly packed to prevent penetration, even by cavalry. The flanks of chariots and cavalry were mobile "wings" that could be used to envelope an enemy charging the center, or used to reinforce the opposite flank if it were attacked. Porus' strategy seems to have been impeccable.

Upon seeing Porus' army, Alexander halted his advance, allowing the infantry time to catch up with him, even catch their breath after a forced march. Then he moved, swiftly. The principal thrust was a cavalry attack, led by about one thousand mounted archers, on Porus' left, with infantry following. As the mounted Greeks moved, Indian cavalry shadowed them until Alexander's forces veered into the Indian lines. At about this time the Greek foot came into play at the rear of the shadowing Indian cavalry. This attracted Indian concern and, foolishly, they turned and attacked the Greeks. This was an unpracticed, awkward maneuver that was militarily ineffective and caused considerable confusion. In battle, confusion once started may be difficult to stop, and so it seems to have been here; things went from bad to worse for Porus' forces. The Indian army's left flank was pushed to the center, crowding the elephants and Indian infantry. The elephants seem to have panicked in the fray and did as much if not more damage to the Indian army in their frenzied stomping than they did to the invading soldiery. Arrian tells us of "much slaughter." In the end Alexander's vigor as a leader and the experience and spirit of his forces carried the day.

Porus, unlike his Persian counterpart Darius, stayed with the battle until it was clearly lost. He then withdrew in an orderly way to tend his wounds and seek refuge. Alexander observed this withdrawal and asked Taxiles to go fetch the king and bring him back unharmed since he had proved himself a brave and noble man on the battlefield. Taxiles and Porus, however, were old sworn enemies, and this could not have been something that Taxiles was anxious to do. So, with some caution we can be sure, Taxiles approached Porus' elephant and hailed his defeated adversary, asking him to halt and hear a message from Alexander. Porus did not trust Taxiles, he turned on him and tried to run him through with a javelin. Clearly, there was still more than a little fight left in the defeated king. This all too human scene was observed by Alexander, who must have sensed that he had somehow picked the wrong man for the job. Alexander therefore asked another Indian ruler, Meroes, who had thrown in his lot with the Greeks, but was an old friend of Porus, to see if he could convince Porus to stop. Meroes succeeded in his task and brought Porus to Alexander.

This meeting between Alexander and Porus is one of the most noble in history. On the one side is a great Indian king, tall and handsome; defeated, true, but with dignity and spirit still in him, who had demonstrated his courage and convictions in a mighty test. On the other side is a youthful king, a military genius who had just won another great victory, but for whom it is simply one more conquest among many, another chip in the gigantic mosaic of the new and growing Macedonian Empire. Arrian reports the following dialogue between these two men:

> Then Alexander first addressing him bade him say what he desired to be done with him. Porus is said to have replied "Treat me, Alexander, like a king." And Alexander, pleased with the reply, answered: "It shall be as you desire, Porus, for my part, do you for your part ask what you desire." He replied that everything was contained in this one request. (Brunt 1983, 2:59)

For this reply and Porus' courage, both here and in battle, Alexander gave him back his sovereignty over all of the Greek conquests in India, apparently on the supposition that it is not possible to treat a man as a king unless he has a kingdom. Thus Alexander brought to an end his last great battle.

Alexander's is certainly one of the most human gestures to have come from war. It also reminds us that he was no ordinary man or military genius, and that is reason enough to recall this splendid story of human adventure and courage.

# Bibliography

M. Andronicos, *Vergina: The Royal Tombs and The Ancient City* (Athens, 1984).

M. M. Austin, *The Hellenistic World from Alexander to the Roman Conquest: A Selection of Ancient Sources in Translation* (Cambridge, 1981).

E. Badian, "Greeks and Macedonians," in B. Barr-Sharrar and E.N. Borza eds., *Macedonia and Greece in Late Classical and Early Hellenistic times*, vol. 10 *(Studies in the History of Art)* (Washington, D.C., 1982).

R.S. Bagnall, *The Administration of the Ptolemaic Territories Outside Egypt* (Leiden, 1976).

———, "Papyrology and Ptolemaic History, 1956-1980," *Classical World* 76, part 1 (1982): 13-21.

B. Barr-Sharrar, "Macedonian Metal Vases in Perspective: Some Observations on Context and Tradition," in *Macedonia and Greece in Late Classical and Early Hellenistic Times* (Washington, D.C., 1982).

M. Bieber, *"Alexander the Great in Greek and Roman Art,"* (Chicago, 1964).

E.N. Borza, "Alexander and the Return from Siwa," *Historia* 16 (1967) 369.

A.B. Bosworth, "Alexander and Ammon," in *Greece and the Ancient Mediterranean in History and Prehistory*, Studies presented to Fritz Schachermeyr, edited by K. Kinzl. (Berlin, 1977).

———, *Conquest and Empire. The Reign of Alexander the Great* (Cambridge, Mass., 1988)

# Bibliography

P.A. Brunt, ed. Arrian, *History of Alexander and Inica*, Loeb Classical Library, I (Cambridge, Mass., and London, 1976); II (1983).

W. Burkert, *Ancient Mystery Cults* (Cambridge, Mass., and London 1987).

G. Cawkwell, *Philip of Macedon* (London and Boston 1978).

N. Davis, & C. M. Kraay, *The Hellenistic Kingdoms, Portrait Coins and History* (London 1973).

W. Dittenberger & K. Purgold, *Olympia*, vol. 5: *Die Inschriften von Olympia* (Berlin 1896).

J.H. Ellis, *Philip II and Macedonian Imperialism* (London 1976).

J. Ferguson, *The Religions of the Roman Empire* (Ithaca 1970).

P.M. Fraser, *Ptolemaic Alexandria* (Oxford 1972).

E.N. Gardiner, *Athletics of the Ancient World* (Oxford 1930).

F.C. Grant, *Hellenistic Religions: The Age of Syncretism* (New York 1953).

P. Green, "The Royal Tombs at Vergina: A Historical Analysis," in W.L. Adams and E.N. Borza eds., *Philip II, Alexander the Great and the Macedonian Heritage* (Washington, D.C. 1982).

N.G.L. Hammond, 1972. *A History of Macedonia*, vol. 1: *Historical Geography and Prehistory* (Oxford 1972).

N.G.L. Hammond, and G.T. Griffith, *History of Macedonia, 550-336 B.C.*, vol. 2 (Oxford 1979).

H.A. Harris, *Greek Athletes and Athletics.* (Bloomington 1966).

H.-V. Herrmann, *Olympia, Heiligtum und Wettkampfstatte* (Munich 1972).

C. Kraay and M. Hirmer, *Greek Coins* (New York 1966).

G. Luck, *Arcana Mundi: Magic and the Occult in the Greek and Roman Worlds* (Baltimore 1985).

A. Mallwitz, *Olympia und Seine Bauten* (Munich 1972).

J.W. McCrindle, *The Invasion of India by Alexander the Great as Described by Arrian, Q. Curtius, Plutarch, and Justin* (Westminster 1896).

S.G. Miller, "The Philippeion and Macedonian Hellenistic Architecture," *AthMitt* (1973) 189.

L. Moretti, *Olympionikai, i vincitori negli antichi agoni Olimpici* (Rome 1957).

N.A.H. Neave, "Faces and Fingerprints," in A.R. David ed., *Mysteries of the Mummies* (London 1978).

———, "The Reconstruction of the Heads and Faces of Three Ancient Egyptians," in A.R. David ed., *The Manchester Museum Mummy Project* (Manchester 1979).

J.J. Pollitt, *Art in the Hellenistic Age* (Cambridge 1986).

A.J.N.W. Prag, J.H. Musgrave & R.A.H. Neave, "The Skull from Tomb II at Vergina: King Philip of Macedon," *Journal of Hellenic Studies* 104 (1984) 60-78.

C. Préaux, *L'Economie royale des Lagides* (Brussels 1939).

J.S. Rhine & C.E.E. Moore, in *Maxwell Museum Technical Series*, vol. 1 (1982).

K. Rhomiopoulou, "An Outline of Macedonian History and Art," in *The Search for Alexander* (Washington D.C. 1980).

C. Rolley, "Une couronne et une diademe sur la tete d'Alexandre," in *Akten der 9. Internationalen Tagung ber Antike Bronzen, Wien...1986.* (Vienna forthcoming).

P. Roos, "Alexander I in Olympia," *Eranos* (1985) 83 162-68.

A. Rowe, *Discovery of the Famous Temple and Enclosure of Serapis at Alexandria* (Cairo 1946).

T.T.B. Ryder, *Koine Eirene: General Peace and Local Independence in Ancient Greece* (Oxford 1965).

A.E. Samuel, "From Athens to Alexandria: Hellenism and Social Goals in Ptolemaic Egypt," *Studia Hellenistica* (1983) 16.

C.T. Seltman, *Greek Coins* (London 1933).

W.W. Tarn, 1948. *Alexander the Great* (Cambridge 1948 and Boston 1956).

*The Search for Alexander*, published by the Greek Ministry of Culture and Sciences (catalog of the exhibition which opened at the National Gallery of Art in November, 1980) (Washington, D.C. 1980).

H.A. Thompson, "Architecture as a Medium of Public Relations Among the Successors of Alexander," *Macedonia and Greece in Late Classical and Early Hellenistic Times.*

R.A. Tomlinson, "The Architectural Context of the Macedonian Vaulted Tombs," *Annual of the British School at Athens* 82 (1987) 305-12.

A. Tronson, "Satyrus the Peripatetic and the Marriages of Philip II," 104 *Journal of Hellenic Studies* (1984) 116-26.

M.J. Vermaseien, *Cybele and Attis: The Myth and the Cult* (London 1977).

F.W. Walbank, *The Hellenistic World* (Cambridge, Mass. 1982).

C.B. Welles, "The Discovery of Sarapis and the Foundation of Alexandria," 11 *Historia* (1962) 271-98.

D. White, "1985 Excavations on Bates' island, Marsa Matruh," 23 *Journal of the American Research Center in Egypt.* (1986) 51-84.

———, "1987 Excavations on Bates' Island, Marsa Matruh: Second Preliminary Report," 26 *Journal of the American Research Center in Egypt* (1989) 87-114.

R.E. Witt, *Isis in the Graeco-Roman World.* (Ithaca 1971).

N.I. Xirotiris & F. Langenscheidt, F. "The Cremations from the Royal Macedonian Tombs of Vergina," *Archaiologike Ephemeris* (1981) 142-60.

## ANCIENT AUTHORS

| | | |
|---|---|---|
| Herodotus | *History* | 5th century B.C. |
| | *Maccabees* | 2d century B.C. |
| Diodorus | *Library of History* | 1st century B.C. |
| Plutarch | *Life of Alexander* | 1st century A.D. |
| Plutarch | *Moralia* | 1st century A.D. |
| Strabo | *Geography* | 1st century A.D. |
| Arrian | *Anabasis* | 2d century A.D. |
| Athenaeus | *Deipnosophistae* | 2d century A.D. |
| Pausanias | *Description of Greece* | 2d century A.D. |
| Philostratus | *Life of Apollonius* | 2d century A.D. |